PERSONAL FINANCE FOR TEENS AND COLLEGE STUDENTS

THE COMPLETE GUIDE TO FINANCIAL LITERACY FOR TEENS AND YOUNG ADULTS

KARA ROSS

PUBLISHING FORTE

INTRODUCTION

One of the reasons poor people are sometimes considered happier than the rich is that they do not have to deal with the guilt and self-blame that comes from the poor handling of funds. Many times, money "passes" through our coffers than stays. The art of saving and planning the use of money is essential and is key to finding peace in life. This should be instilled in our lives at a very young age so that even when we are old, we will look back and smile at our financial journey. It is good to never worry about money because you will have amassed enough to cover your needs. It is everyone's dream to achieve financial freedom earlier rather than later.

It is often said that money—whatever the amount—can never be enough, but there sure should be a ceiling to that statement. Some simple things can be done today to better your financial situation tomorrow. Unfortunately, most people only realize this late, when many years have been wasted, and there isn't much that can be done to better the situation. This book is meant to teach young people to manage their finances and build sizable financial knowledge from a very young age.

Sources of income differ from individual to individual. Some people get into jobs at very young ages and have paychecks coming in. Some may be earning dividends, getting royalties, and other varying sources of income. As young adults, the urge is usually to spend the money and live "the life." While that may be the 'in thing", being wise with your money helps you in the long run. The future depends on today.

Your personal finances are crucial to you, especially in our current economic times. It is important to know as much as you can about managing your money. You want to be armed with as much information to help you stay on track with your finances. It may be difficult, but perseverance, determination, consistency, and educating yourself will assist you in making it through.

Maybe you want to avoid drowning in debt after seeing people falling into the trap, but you don't know how to go about it. The more you try to avoid debt, the more challenging it becomes.

You probably aren't managing your money well because you don't have any prior money-management experience. Sadly, after several attempts to get vital money-management tips online, you end up with nothing, and you feel help isn't ever coming your way. Maybe you've started applying some financial strategies but don't know if they can help you attain your financial goals. Again, you probably have some bucks but don't know what to do with them. Perhaps you hope to save some money to reach a particular goal, but you don't know how much to save, weekly or monthly, to achieve your objective.

Just imagine how you'd feel knowing that you could avoid debt by saving more money. You wouldn't struggle to become a self-made millionaire if you knew the right strategies to manage your money. Maybe you wouldn't struggle to save sufficient money to attain your financial goal if someone had shown you investment accounts to grow your money.

My passion for helping teens and college students secure their future and finances birthed this book. The lessons I've learnt about money are massive, and they're presented in this book. I am about to tell you the tricks I used to regulate my finances and avert the headaches of living paycheck to paycheck. I hope you practice the tips within and reap the benefits; I'm sure they will help you manage your money and prepare for future financial obligations. With the help of this book, you can attain your money goal.

This guide is not only a mirror through which you see yourself in the future but a handy informant on how to get there. Dreaming alone is not enough. One has to act to bring the dream to fruition. This book's guidelines will help you start acting today for the life you want to live tomorrow. You do not want to look back at your young life and say, "If only I had known."

Your journey to being successful with money starts with planning, which is our focus in Chapter One. I hope you enjoy it.

1

PLAN AHEAD

It's been a long time since I finished high school, but the experiences of those days still linger in my mind. I remember how indecision almost cost me an entire academic session. My father would credit my account twice in the space of two weeks: the first credit was to settle all my educational needs, including my school fees, while the second would address my personal needs.

I DIDN'T HAVE any problem with my academic needs. The school usually addressed that as soon as each student paid their fees. So, I quickly listed my personal needs; I knew I would purchase some clothes and a pair of boots.

THE FIRST BATCH of credit came in as expected a few days before resumption. And, since payment of school fees could be made within the first four weeks of resumption, I went for my personal needs first. A week later, my father lost his job, and I was on the verge of losing an academic session.

. . .

I wasn't my old self. Regrets were written all over me, and I felt that my whole world had crumbled. Two of my two closest friends knew that I was distraught. They asked the cause of my problem, and I told them everything. Eventually, they helped me with some money, and I was able to pay my school fees. I owe them my life.

Lack of planning can negatively impact your ability to grow your money and manage it appropriately. So, this chapter will focus on budgeting, different budgeting methods, what to include in your budgets, and a few budgeting tips to make the right money decisions. If you can't account for how you spend your money, or you're struggling to manage your finances, get your budget; the budget will pitch your income against your expenditure and expose the items you're spending money on. Again, it can help you determine the amount to save or invest.

Budgeting is critical to financial freedom. If you don't have a budget, you can't be successful with money. As a spending plan, the budget pays keen attention to current and future income and expenditure.

Core Reasons Why Successful People Create Budgets

Do you feel like spending all the money you earn? No problem; most teens and college students do. But that is not the best way to live. You attain financial freedom by saving and investing your money, not by spending it. Little wonder that experts say you need a budget to manage your finances efficiently (Bell, 2021).

. . .

HERE ARE the benefits of creating a budget and sticking to it:

1. Identifies your long-term goals and adheres you to them.

Do you hope to purchase a house, buy a car or take a trip to Paris, Dubai, New York, or some other beautiful cities worldwide? Fine, but you won't achieve any of these long-term goals if you aimlessly spend your money on every attractive item you encounter.

BUT YOU WON'T HAVE any problem if you have an operational budget. The budget will force you to concentrate on your goals, save money, track your progress and achieve your dreams.

IT IS painful to know that you won't be purchasing your favorite Xbox game or cashmere sweater, but when you remember that you are saving to buy a house or a car, you will gladly leave the store with nothing.

2. Helps you avoid unnecessary debts.

DON'T ALLOW anything or anyone to make you spend more than you can spare. Some people accumulate credit card debt because they can't take their eyes off certain items when they shop in stores and other marketplaces. It would make sense that, according to one study, in 2020, the average American household had credit card debts of $7,027 (Bell, 2021).

YOU WON'T HAVE to worry about unnecessary debts if you have a budget and follow it; you will know how to balance your income and expenditure. Again, instead of wallowing in debts, you will be saving toward your short-term and long-term goals. So, this time next year, your spend-happy pals and colleagues will be visiting debt counselors while you're getting ready to move into a new house, drive a new car, or jet off to your favorite destination.

3. Prepares you for the future.

IT'S okay if you stick to your budget, spend wisely, and never accumulate any credit card debt, but don't forget that you will need to save more money to secure your future.

MAKE investment contributions an aspect of your budget, and you will have a financially secured future. How? Channel a particular percentage of your income into your 401(k), IRA, or other retirement plans. It doesn't matter if you have to cut down some expenses to secure your future.

4. Helps you deal with emergencies.

UNEXPECTED SITUATIONS like layoffs from work, sickness, injury, and divorce can be sources of your financial problem. You can't deal with these situations if you don't have an emergency fund.

YOU ARE PROTECTED from these emergencies if you have an operating budget. The budget will create room for the emergency fund. Financial experts say that an ideal emergency fund would cover three to six months of your expenses. The fund will help you avoid financial crises and unnecessary debt.

RAISING it will take some time, but don't be tempted to move a significant part of your income there. Instead, grow the fund slowly by adding a consistent amount –$10 or $20 each week.

5. Exposes negative spending habits.

I'M sure you've heard something about impulse buying. It happens when you purchase items you barely need – and that's fine; a recent study revealed that most teens and young adults spend money on items they don't need. But such habits can prevent you from reaching your financial goals.

IF YOU WANT to monitor your spending habits, budget your finances. A budget will focus your attention on your financial goals, not just your spending habits.

CREATE a budget if you want to control your money; otherwise, should it go the other way, you will have many threatening financial problems to deal with. Make sure to design your budget since you wouldn't want to lose control over your money. If you are struggling with saving and want to be free, create a budget.

Top Money-Saving Tricks For Teens And College Students

Many young people have difficulties saving money. Some would gladly spend every buck they see or earn because they often think cash will continue to flow in endlessly. They hardly recognize that unforeseen circumstances could cause them financial difficulties in the future.

DON'T BE LIKE THEM. Instead, set aside some money weekly or monthly. The little money you save will surely do your world some good. Sure, it may not now, but you will use the savings soon enough. Use these simple money-saving tricks to attain future financial success:

1. Create a budget.

IT IS SIMPLE: you can't save if you don't have a budget. Again, an allocation doesn't guarantee your success with money if you fail to stick to it.

A BUDGET SHOULDN'T STOP you from having fun or enjoying your life; it only helps you decide how to spend your money and what percentage should go toward entertainment, bills, savings, and other things you might want to achieve.

.   .   .

You CAN USE *MyMoney* or any other online mobile banking app to monitor your income and expenditure.

2. Save and invest your money.

RIGHT NOW, you may be facing some challenges in saving and investing. Don't allow the obstacles to stop you from keeping a few dollars aside every week. Soon, maybe even after a year or two, the amount you have saved will amaze you. A careful assessment of your budget will show you how much you can channel into your savings account every month.

DEAL with the investing part by asking whether your employer has a 401(k) account, then decide the percentage to contribute from your salary. You are free to increase your future contributions.

IT's okay if your employer doesn't offer the 401(k) retirement plan: you can opt for a Roth IRA. Self-employed people can also take advantage of the IRA retirement package.

3. Save one-third of your income.

No AMOUNT of money is too small to save. But experts say that you should strive to keep one-third of your income if you want to attain financial freedom in no distant time. For them, you will cope with future financial difficulties – like unforeseen expenses, layoffs, or home and car repairs – if you can save $1 out of each $3 you earn. Does that look difficult or even impossible? There's no obstacle you can't crush if you believe. Just cut some of the items you spend money on to increase your savings.

4. Start an emergency fund.

UNFORESEEN EXPENSES CAN EXPOSE you to financial hardship, especially if you don't have an emergency fund. Identify a high-interest money market or savings account, and put some money there. Then, should you have any future financial problems, you know where to get the money. Financial experts say that your emergency fund should be up to your three to six months' expenses.

5. Pay off your debts.

SAVING CAN BE a great way of securing the future, but don't allow your debt profile to grow just because you are trying to save some money. Pay off every penny you owe if you hope to attain financial freedom someday. Debt can cause you serious financial issues, especially when you need a loan to set up a business or make a substantial purchase. It can have negative impacts on your creditworthiness.

IF YOU FOLLOW these tricks wholeheartedly, you won't believe the amount you'll save in the next few months.

· · ·

IF YOU WANT to be successful with money, you can learn and apply a few financial skills.

Financial Skills Every Young Adult Must Have

If you are displaying any financial skills right now, I want you to know that you were not born with them. Over time, you can learn a few financial skills through mistakes, but you surely need more than your current skills to be successful with money.

EVERY TEEN and college student must have these financial skills, according to the Take Charge America Team (n.d.):

1. Basic budgeting.

GETTING to know how to plan or structure a budget is key to financial freedom. It is a skill you must have as a teenager. A budget shows your income, expenditure, and items you are spending money on. You don't have to sweat over it since tons of mobile budgeting apps you could use. Again, most of these apps are free and available for download on the *Apple* and *Play* stores.

2. Bank account basics.

YOU NEED to understand a few banking basics like overdrafts, overdraft fees, minimum balance requirements, and service fees. You will learn everything about banking in the next chapter.

3. Wants versus needs.

GET to know the differences and similarities between wants and needs as soon as possible. The concept of needs and wants is quite simple, just like budgeting, yet you can easily misinterpret them if you are not careful enough.

NEEDS COVER basic things you would use to sustain your life, such as food, clothes, shelter, and education. *Wants* are other desires, like video games and books. Wants must wait when money is tight.

4. Saving for emergencies.

TEENS AND COLLEGE students may not have a fully funded, ready-to-go emergency savings account yet. But, the earlier they know to prepare for unexpected medical bills, job loss, major car repairs, or other true emergencies, the better for them. It would be best to start saving money for potential future troubles.

5. Positive credit history.

. . .

YOU CAN EASILY ACCOMPLISH your future financial goals if you start developing or building a good credit history right now. Just know that credit card debt and other financial mistakes you make today can threaten your future financial goals. Pay all your bills in full and on time if you hope to have a clean credit history. We will discuss this more in Chapter Four.

6. Know that nothing is guaranteed.

THAT JOB you cherish so much can disappear in no time; nothing is guaranteed in this life. So, start preparing for undesirable circumstances right now, so you won't feel the impacts of misfortune when they strike. And, what's the best way you can prepare? Start saving money.

7. Understand when to get help.

TEENS AND COLLEGE students are prone to financial mistakes, just as are older generations. Some of these mistakes can be too big for you to handle, especially with the economy as it is. Still, help is just a block or two away; student loan counseling and credit counseling may be all you need to avoid an imminent financial mess.

GET familiar with these skills or face a severe monetary crisis. If you have a budget and stick to it, you will have few or no financial challenges to deal with. However, according to James (2021), the success of a budget depends on some specific issues.

Logical Things to Do Before You Create a Budget

Evaluate your financial goals and priorities before you create your budget. If you aren't doing this, you will have the wrong budget and failed dreams (James, 2021). These fundamental issues will determine the fate of your budget:

- *Purpose of the budget:* What's motivating you to create a budget? Is it because you want to purchase a house, buy a car, pay off a debt or save for retirement? If the reason isn't tangible, creating the budget and sticking to it will become very difficult. Wait a moment and reflect on what's motivating you to make that budget.
- *Significance of financial goals:* It's okay if you have many goals to reach. But, if you hope to come up with outstanding budgets, rank your financial objectives according to their importance. For example, if you want to purchase a house, buy a car, pay off debt and save for retirement, rank the goals and focus on them one after the other. If two or more goals happen to have an equal level of importance, try handling them simultaneously.
- *Budget goals' deadlines:* A deadline can make a financial goal look concrete and motivate you to attain the goal. Let's say you want to save $100,000 in your 401(k) or Roth IRA in five years; a deadline will help you figure out how much to contribute each month, to reach the goal. Again, if you set a deadline for a financial goal, you can quickly identify the expenses you need to cut to attain the goal.
- *Expenses to cut in the budget:* Identify the payments you need to cut to achieve your financial goals. For

example, instead of patronizing eateries, pack your lunch at home – that's going to save you some extra bucks. Don't wait until you develop the budget before you create a list of expenses to cut. This is a way to make each dollar count.

- *Erratic areas of the budget:* People have spending issues: some hate cooking their food at home, whereas others are addicted to shopping; some have a hard time avoiding impulse purchases in supermarkets and grocery stores. What's your harmful spending habit? Identify it and find a way to deal with it. Let's say restaurant dinners are draining your savings: start cooking at home. If you are addicted to shopping and impulse purchases, work on your mindset. Prioritize your needs, not your wants.

Reasonable Tips on How to Budget Your Money

Create a budget to regulate expenses, boost savings and attain your financial goals. Use budgeting apps or simple spreadsheets to make a budget; *Personal Capital, Count About, Digit, PocketSmith, Money Patrol,* and *Trim* are amazing budgeting apps that you can utilize to develop a budget, according to Barret (2021).

Pay attention to these tips because they will guide you through the budget creation process (Vohwinkle, 2021):

1. Compile your financial statements.

. . .

GET your financial statements before you start designing your budget. Such information may include investment accounts, credit card bills, bank statements, mortgage loan statements, and recent utility bills. The statement will show everything about your income and expenditure, especially where your money is going. So, if you're overspending on certain items, you will see it as soon as you get your financial statement.

2. Compute your income.

HOW MUCH DO you earn per month? If your income isn't fixed, pay attention to what flows in every month. Still, your baseline income could be the least that you made in the previous year. Let's say the lowest income you had in the last year was $1500. Go ahead and adopt it as your income.

3. List your monthly expenses.

STATE THE PAYMENTS you hope to make in a month. Such expenses may include insurance, savings, student loans, groceries, travel, utilities, personal care, and transportation costs. If you are struggling to identify the items you spend money on, your credit card statements, receipts, and bank statements for the last three months can be of help.

4. Differentiate between fixed and variable expenses.

.   .   .

MANDATORY EXPENSES LIKE CAR PAYMENTS, trash pickup, internet service, and rent or mortgage payments are fixed expenses; most of the time, the amount you pay for this basic stuff doesn't change. Should you want to save a particular percentage of your income monthly, add this amount to your fixed expenses.

IN CONTRAST, variable expenses aren't constant. They include fees on groceries, gifts, entertainment, and gasoline.

DETERMINE the amount to spend on each category each month. Survey your bank transactions for the last three months to get a rough spending estimate on your fixed and variable expenses.

5. Aggregate your income and expenses separately.

IT's okay if your income is more than your expenses. Create a 401(k) or Roth IRA account and put the extra money there. You can also use the funds to pay off your debts (if you have any).

IF YOUR INCOME is less than your expenses, you should find a way to trim your costs.

6. Modify your expenses.

CUT some of your variable expenses when your expenses are more than your income. For example, if you eat out three or four times a week, reduce it to one. You could also terminate any memberships you don't use or take advantage of.

CONSIDER CUTTING some of your fixed expenses if you're not getting the desired results when slicing your variable costs.

7. Define your budget plan.

BIEBER (2018) RECOMMENDS that you consider your financial goal before settling for any budget plan. For example, a program that works fine for someone trying to purchase a house may not be suitable for someone who wants to save for retirement. Here are the major budget plans:

- *Zero-based budget:* Dave Ramsey made this budget approach famous; it ensures that earnings equal expenses. In other words, each dollar you earn fixes something. A zero-based budget doesn't mean that you won't be saving any money at all; it's just that all expenses are fixed and restrictive. Use this budget plan to avoid overspending, reduce or pay off debt and attain your financial goals.
- *Line-item or traditional budget:* People with spending issues or those struggling to pay off their debts can opt for this budget plan. Just write out all your expenses and categorize them into estimated, actual, and leftover expenses. Compare cumulative fees or payments with your income and use the *Tiller* app to run the process efficiently. You can then slice any expenses you consider irrelevant or unnecessary.

- *Proportional budgets:* "80/20", "50/30/20", and other budgets with loose guidelines are examples of balanced budgets. For example, anyone who adopts the 80/20 budget would spend 80 percent of their earnings and save 20 percent. Elizabeth Warren developed the 50/30/20 budget plan, in which 50 percent of revenue will be spent on your needs, 30 percent on wants, and 20 percent on savings. While needs are basic life necessities, wants aren't. Needs include rent, food, and shelter, while wants are generally entertainment-based. What happens if these budget plans do not work for you? Modify the 50/30/20 plan until you come up with a plan suitable for your financial goals.
- *Compensate yourself first:* Here's a saving model that could be used to reach a saving goal. Let's say you want to save $5,000 in the next six months, and you're using this model. At the dawn of a new month, you would remove the money you want to save before making any expenses. How much do you want to save per month? Is it 5, 10, or 20 percent of your income? What if you can't sustain the figure you come up with? You can always slice your expenses.
- *Envelope Budget:* Tends to shape how you use cash. Let's say your expense categories are transportation, groceries, and entertainment – you have to specify the amount to assign for each category. Withdraw money from the A.T.M. and address the items one after the other. Just know that you can't spend more, even if the cash isn't sufficient for the expense categories.

I recommend this budget plan for people with spending issues.

REMEMBER, no multipurpose budget plan; everything depends on the financial goals you want to accomplish.

LET'S assume you earn $4,000 each month. If you want each dollar to fix something, a zero-based budget would be applicable. The budget could look like this:

Payment	Monthly Budget
House down-payment fund	$450
Retirement savings	$600
Christmas fund	$30
Emergency fund	$80
Travel fund	$100
Car payment	$250
Insurance premiums	$200
Rent	$1,000

Utilities	$300
Entertainment	$150
Groceries	$400
Gas and vehicle maintenance	$300
Wiggle room	$40
Cellphone	$50
Clothing	$50
Total	**$4,000**

8. Select the right tool.

. . .

SIMPLY USE an Excel spreadsheet or any budgeting app to design your budget. There are several budgeting apps to download on the Play Store and Apple Store.

HOW DO you want to budget your money? The decision is all yours. Still, you need to know the right items to add to your budget.

Logical Items to Include in Your Budget

Like other people, you might be tempted to focus more on mortgage payments, grocery costs, and other monthly bills when designing your budget. Still, if you don't create room for unexpected expenses, you may end up with an inefficient allocation (Caldwell, 2020).

AN OPERATING BUDGET must include the following expenses:

1. Living expenses:

WE INCUR CERTAIN EXPENSES DAILY. Such costs may include payments on transportation, rent, feeding, and other utilities.

2. Monthly debt:

IS THERE any debt to repay monthly? It could be a student loan or a credit card debt. If there's any debt to repay monthly, make sure your budget covers it.

. . .

3. Annual payments:

CERTAIN PAYMENTS, like car, taxes, registration, and property taxes, need to be paid yearly or twice a year. You will have problems making these payments if your budget doesn't address them. Determine the aggregate amount of the previous year's payment, then divide it by twelve to know the amount to save each month.

4. Emergency fund:

THE EMERGENCY FUND can protect you from unexpected repairs, loss of jobs, and other emergencies.

5. Fun activities:

CREATE a list of the activities you enjoy doing and state their costs. Such activities may include video games, going to the gym, or a night out with friends. Still, please make sure the activities are in their order of importance.

6. Donations and gifts:

SET some money aside for gifts and donations.

. . .

A REASONABLE BUDGET has these items. If you are working with an operational budget, you will soon reach your goal. Still, you should be ready to trial, survey, and modify your financial goals from time to time, or you likely won't reach them.

Tracking, Reviewing, and Adjusting Your Budget

Track and review your expenses to see whether you are making the right financial decisions. If it seems your budget can't accommodate your goals, adjust it. Here's how to do it:

1. Record all expenses.

I ALREADY SHOWED you six categories of expenses to include your budget. Total your monthly expenses to curb over-spending and other spending issues. Again, the budgeting app or spreadsheet used to design the budget can track and review it for you.

2. Monitor your spending.

SET a spending limit for each category. As soon as you hit the limit for a class, focus on the next one. If you aren't monitoring your spending habits, you won't attain your financial goals.

3. Analyze your budget regularly.

.   .   .

EVALUATE your budget from time to time to see if it is compatible with your financial goals and current realities. Certain life situations could impact your spending priorities and income; regular budget analysis can help you spot these situations and address them before they threaten your goals.

JUST MAKE sure your budget is working for you; should it go south, change or adjust it.

IF YOU WANT to create a fantastic budget for your goal, these budgeting cues will help:

- Save aggressively if your work is based on commission. The market might slow down a bit in the coming days.
- Divide your salary by weeks if you earn monthly to prevent cash flow issues. You can save the cash for the remaining weeks in a secure account.
- Modify your budget monthly to prevent overestimated or underestimated expenses.
- Focus on your savings goals if your income is more than your expenses. Don't boost your spending yet.
- Be budget-conscious daily. If something isn't on your budget for the day, don't spend money on it.

Start planning how to be successful with money now. As you already know, a lack of planning can harm your ability to grow your money and manage it appropriately. That's why this chapter explored budgeting, different ways of budgeting, what to include in a realistic budget, and a few budgeting tips to make the right money decisions.

. . .

BUT, you won't get anywhere if you fail to understand the basics of banking, which will be our focus in the next chapter.

2

BANKING AND SAVING

The previous chapter explored budgeting, what to include in a realistic budget, and a few budgeting tips that you can exploit to make the right money decisions. Here, you will learn the basics of banking and why holding bank accounts remains crucial to personal finance.

I WAS thirteen years old when my dad started giving me an extra $10 each week, telling me: "Kara, you can have this." I gladly took the money and spent it because I knew another $10 would be up for grabs the following week. After all, that was my little paycheck, I always told myself. The paycheck continued for a year.

THEN ONE DAY, after Dad had stopped offering me the stipend, he called me to his room and asked how much I had saved of the $520 I received from him in the past year. I told him I had spent it all, though I couldn't recollect how the money was spent.

. . .

MAYBE THAT WOULDN'T HAVE HAPPENED if I'd had a bank account. A bank account can help you define your expenses, save more money and attain your financial goals.

Benefits of Having a Bank Account

If you have a bank account, you can quickly evaluate your spending habits, cut unnecessary expenses, save more money, and reach your financial goals.

A BANK ACCOUNT is so easy to open that anyone can have one, provided they have a passport, state-issued I.D. card, or driver's license. It's okay if you don't have a bank account yet; just head straight to any bank with your proof of identification.

HERE ARE the significant benefits of having a bank account:

1. Accurate financial history.

YOU WILL HAVE DETAILED information about how your money is spent if you have a bank account. Each credit app you use won't work unless you link them with your bank account.

AGAIN, if there is any negative bank account information for you, it will reflect on your credit report. You will learn more about credit reports in Chapter Four.

. . .

2. Safety.

EVERYONE WANTS to keep their money where it is safe. You may be tempted to store the money you save in your house, but you will lose it if there is a fire or robbery in your home. Instead, open a bank account and save your money there. Since each bank account is insured, you won't lose a dime if the bank is robbed.

3. Convenience of transactions.

EACH BANK ACCOUNT comes with a debit card or checkbook, so you can issue payments via your card. You don't have to load your wallet with cash because you will have to purchase a few items. Again, you can use your bank's mobile app to make payments from the comfort of your home.

COMPARE the fees and interest rates charged by banks in your area when you finally decide to open an account. If there are any account options tagged "budget checking" or "student," opt for such accounts, because they will have low or no fees.

HOW CAN you know the correct bank account to open?

Bank Account Options for Teens and College Students

Banks offer tons of account options for their customers. However, a bank account can be a blessing or a curse. Pay attention to your financial goal before opening any bank account.

All you need to make a sound judgment might be a few bank account tips.

So, let's discuss bank accounts:

1. Savings accounts.

MULLER (2020) RECOMMENDS PUTTING your money into a savings account if you need to save to pay your college dues, purchase a car or attain other financial goals. You can grow your money when you put it in a savings account. Simply set up a conventional savings account in any local bank.

AGAIN, there are several online savings accounts you could opt for—for example, Google *"online savings accounts in Chicago"* if that's where you live.

SAVINGS ACCOUNTS USUALLY ATTRACT a certain amount of interest monthly.

2. Checking accounts.

ONE THING I forgot to say about savings accounts is that you can't access them at any time, unlike checking accounts, which can be accessed via checks, debit cards, and your bank's A.T.M.

. . .

ALTHOUGH CHECKING accounts can offer terrific cash reliefs, minimize your spending by keeping transaction invoices and records. These records can help you track your expenses and decide what to cut to balance your finances.

LINK your savings and checking accounts together to avert overdraft charges and transfer money quickly from one to another.

3. Money market accounts (M.M.A.).

MULLER (2020) STATES that money market accounts are similar to savings accounts; you put money into both types and earn interest. But, the interest earned via a money market account is higher than that of a savings account.

SINCE THE MINIMUM balance requirement of an M.M.A. is very high, it may be out of your reach. Their higher minimum balance requirement ensures that account holders earn huge annual percentage yield (A.P.Y.).

4. Certificate of deposit.

THIS IS money you deposit for a specific time, and it usually generates more interest than savings and checking accounts. Fernando and Anderson (2021) advise that banks and credit unions offer their customers certificates of deposit. Your financial goal should help you decide the appropriate account option to create.

Prominent Bank Account Terms to Know

If you are planning to open a bank account, that's fine. But, even if your parents got one for you in the past, you still need to understand how banks work and the various terms they use to communicate with their customers (Murakami-Fester, 2020). So, I will explain some banking terms, one after the other:

1. A.P.Y. (annual percentage yield).

THIS IS the interest you gain on your deposit over one year, including compound interest. Banks encourage you to save with them by paying you the A.P.Y.

2. A.P.R. (annual percentage rate).

A.P.R. IS the interest you gain on your deposits for one year. However, it doesn't include compound interest.

3. Banks vs. Credit Unions.

BOTH BANKS and credit unions can operate online or in a concrete building. They offer basic transactions such as deposits, withdrawals, buying and selling securities, and similar transactions. Although banks are profit-oriented financial institutions, credit unions aren't.

. . .

4. Minimum balance requirement.

THIS IS the minimum amount your account must have at all times. For example, if the minimum balance requirement of your bank is $100, and you have $850 in there, you can't withdraw more than $750.

5. Available balance.

THIS IS a fraction of the money in your account, which can be used, withdrawn, or transferred to other accounts. It isn't necessarily the total balance in the account minus the minimum balance requirement.

6. Insufficient funds.

THIS SIMPLY MEANS that the amount you want to withdraw or the payment you intend to make is more than the funds available in your account.

7. E.F.T. (electronic funds transfer).

E.F.T. OCCURS when you do cashless banking operations. Such transactions include automatic bill payments and money transfers via A.T.M.

·   ·   ·

8. Overdraft.

THIS OCCURS when you withdraw more than your available balance. Issue a check to withdraw the excess funds. This option is available for people with overdraft accounts.

9. Routing number.

THIS IS a nine-digit number that specifies your bank. A large bank with branches across several geographic locations can have many routing numbers, so the routing number you use will depend on where you opened the account.

10. F.D.I.C. (Federal Deposit Insurance Corporation).

THE F.D.I.C. ENSURES THAT CUSTOMERS' bank deposits are insured up to $250,000. So, if the bank fails, the customers won't face any financial issues.

11. Cashier's check.

A CASHIER'S check is available for purchase at your bank. It doesn't bounce when used to make payments.

12. Canceled check.

. . .

YOU CAN'T USE A CANCELED check for any other transactions because it has been endorsed and changed to an account.

13. Debit card.

YOUR BANK WILL ISSUE you a debit card against the funds in your account. You don't have to visit the bank to make payments or withdraw money from your account. Use the card to withdraw cash at the nearest A.T.M. or purchase goods and services online.

NO BANKING TERM should sound strange to you anymore.Still, there are a few bank fees to familiarize yourself with, as well.

Common Bank Fees to Avoid

Banks charge their customers specific service fees. Compiled by Gravier (2021), these include:

1. Maintenance or service fee.

BANKS OFTEN CHARGE their customers a monthly service or maintenance fee – such fees can be between $4 and $25. However, you can avoid this fee. How? Open a checking and savings account in the same bank, and maintain the minimum balance.

. . .

IF YOU CAN'T RUN a checking and savings account concurrently in the same bank, try to get bank accounts with no or very little monthly charges.

2. Out-of-network A.T.M. fee.

IF YOU USE NON-NETWORK A.T.M.s, your bank may charge you between $2.50 and $5 per transaction. Use your bank's mobile app to discover fee-free A.T.M.s nearby if you hope to avoid the out-of-network A.T.M. fee.

SHOULD you need to make any withdrawals with no in-network A.T.M.s, opt for a more considerable amount since the out-of-network fee is a one-time payment.

3. Transaction fee.

EACH SAVINGS ACCOUNT holder can do six free transfers and withdrawals per month; excess transfers or withdrawals are charged between $3 and $25 per transaction. If you have a checking account, use it for your daily transactions to avoid transaction fees.

4. Overdraft fee.

IT IS okay to withdraw more than you have in your bank account – just be aware that you might be charged up to $35 for every overdraft. To avoid paying the overdraft fee, set up an automatic direct deposit for the account. After all, if there's sufficient money in the account, you won't need to do an overdraft.

5. Returned item or insufficient fund fee.

IF THE FUNDS in your account can't cover your transaction, your bank will charge you. A returned item or insufficient fund fee could be up to $35 per transaction.

CONSIDER the amount in your account before making any transactions. Consider opting for notifications so that you get an automatic update on your account balance.

6. Wire transfer fee.

YOUR BANK WILL PROBABLY CHARGE you when transferring funds to other bank accounts; depending on the geographical location of the receiving accounts, you may be charged between $16 and $35 per transaction, so don't use wire transfers often. Do a wire transfer when the transaction is official, and the amount is enormous.

7. Account closing fee.

· · ·

IF YOU DECIDE to close your account, make sure it tallies with your bank's rule on a timeline or risk a $25 early account closing fee. Each bank has its own timeline, which could be between 90 and 180 days.

IT IS best to verify your bank's timeline rule at the point of opening the account. Though, on most occasions, you probably wouldn't have opened an account intentionally only for a short period.

MOST OF THESE fees might be relatively small, but if recurring and unnecessary, they can threaten the financial stability of your bank account. You may need to consider the fees charged by banks in your area before you open a bank account.

FOLLOWING ARE a few tips on how to select a bank.

Creative Advice on How to Select a Bank

There are enough options for people who want to open a bank account; you could opt for credit unions, national banks, community banks, or digital-only banks. If you have any bank in mind already, just make sure that the bank offers services that fit your needs. Lambarena (2018) is here to guide you through the process of selecting a bank:

- *Check available account types:* We've already discussed the account options in most financial institutions. Still, if you need all the account options in one bank, I suggest you opt for a big national bank.

- *Fees and rates*: Banks tend to charge their customers for A.T.M. use, monthly maintenance, paper statements, money transfer, and overdrafts, while credit unions –non-profit financial institutions – pay higher A.P.Y. than traditional banks. Additionally, their fees are considerably lower than those of conventional banks. Also, since online banks don't keep physical branches, they have better terms than most traditional banks. So, analyze the fees and rates of these financial institutions before you open your account.
- *A.T.M.s and branches*: Consider your preferences and lifestyle. Would you prefer face-to-face transactions to a phone or online service? Do you travel a lot or need to withdraw cash whenever you are on a journey? Stipulate your needs, and check whether the bank has enough A.T.M.s and branches in the places you often visit. National banks have wider-spread branches and more A.T.M.s. Allpoint, Star, and some credit unions have extensive A.T.M. coverage. Opt for a mobile-only or online bank if you always do digital transactions.
- *Must-have technology:* You don't have to step into a branch before you track or transfer money; technology has made this a reality. But does your prospective bank have its own app? If they do, is it user-friendly? The app should have basic features like security measures, automated savings plans, and budgeting tools. Online and national banks all have the latest technology.
- *Safety:* Keep your money where it will be safe. Open your accounts with banks that are certified by the Federal Deposit Insurance Corporation (F.D.I.C.). Should you decide to use a credit union, opt for

those backed by the National Credit Union Administration (N.C.U.A.). Such banks and credit unions are insured. Check the N.C.U.A. and F.D.I.C. websites to see the list of insured financial institutions.

So, what do you need to open a bank account? Most banks require you to come in with a social security number, a government-issued identity card (S.S.N.), and your first deposit fund. No problem if you don't have an S.S.N.; you can use your tax I.D. number instead. However, if that doesn't work, look for banks that approve passports or other official I.D.s.

Do you want to apply in person? Verify the I.D. type the bank accepts first. If you apply online, the bank might ask you to send them certain pieces of the information via mail, email, or fax.

THE BANK WILL PROCESS your paperwork as soon as it receives it. Processing might take a few days or weeks, but you will get a welcome package by mail if your application is successful. Usually, the package should contain a debit card, PIN, and some complimentary checks.

Reading and Reconciling Your Bank Statements

If you own a savings or checking account in any financial institution, expect a monthly or quarterly bank statement. You are getting a bank statement because your account is still very active. Banks often send the report via mail or email.

· · ·

WHAT EXACTLY IS A BANK STATEMENT?

IT SHOWS YOUR DEPOSITS, transfers, withdrawals, and other transactions. A bank statement will display your starting and ending balances for the period it covers, as well as your bank's contact information. Should there be any financial discrepancies, a bank statement can reconcile the differences. You can use your bank statement to track and trim your expenses.

HOW DO you read a bank statement? Payne (2020) advises that bank statements aren't tricky or difficult to understand. Each bank may customize its reports, but this is the likely information you will see:

1. Basic information.

A BANK'S statement should have the bank's name, mailing address, phone number, and other relevant information.

2. Personal information.

THE STATEMENT SHOULD CARRY your name and contact information.

3. Statement period.

. . .

A BANK STATEMENT covers a specific period, so expect to see the dates there. While some banks use particular days of the month, others will start from the first day and end on the last.

4. Starting and ending balances.

CHECK your balances to know whether you are progressing or regressing financially over the period.

5. Transactions.

THIS SECTION MAKES up information on deposits, checks written, withdrawals, A.C.H. transfers, A.T.M. withdrawals, direct deposits, and pending transactions.

6. Fees.

CHARGED fees will reflect on your monthly bank statement.

7. Interest earned.

THE STATEMENT WILL SHOW the interest you've earned (if there is any). Assuming you have savings or checking accounts in one bank, they will show up on a single statement.

. . .

YOU HAVE JUST LEARNED how to read a bank statement. I will now teach you what to do to reconcile your bank statement.

RECONCILING a bank statement comes with several healthy financial benefits and ensures no issues with your bank transactions. It can help you trail the previous month's uncashed checks and prevent missed or double payments; it also improves money management.

HERE IS how to reconcile your bank statement:

- Compare your bank statement with your financial records to see any deposit, withdrawal, or transfer mistakes.
- Check whether the balance on your bank statement tallies with what your records display. Are there any disparities? Fix them.
- Analyze the deposits shown on your bank statement to see whether they correlate with your records.
- Compare the listed withdrawals on your bank statement with your records.
- Check if there are any discrepancies between your checkbook and bank statement. Then, compare the figures there to your records.

Are there any figure disparities? Fix the problem. Approach your bank if you think something is wrong with the statement.

FINDING an error on a bank statement can be annoying. If you must fix the problem, here are the proper steps to take:

. . .

1. Verify the error.

IF SOMETHING SEEMS wrong or implausible in your bank statement, confirm it first. If possible, identify the proof because it may be all you have to show the bank to rectify the problem.

2. Contact your bank.

REACH out to your bank as soon as you discover the error; you can call the bank's customer service unit or send them an email update. Don't forget to send the proof.

3. Contact the third party.

SHOULD the error involve another party, don't hesitate to inform them. They have to work on their records and resolve the problem as soon as possible.

4. Adjust your records.

MODIFY your records to tally with your bank's corrections. Always try to note the identities of the people you talked to while fixing the issues.

THERE ARE no bank issues that cannot be reconciled. Just take your time to identify the cause(s) of the problem and find a way to fix it. You can usually do this with a call to your bank's customer service unit to solve any issues.

HAVE you ever felt like you don't need a bank account? If so, I highly recommend reconsidering because there are such beautiful benefits to holding a bank account.

THIS CHAPTER EXPLORED every banking detail you need to know to be successful with money. Still, you need to understand mindful spending if you ever hope to reach any of your financial goals. No problem at all, because that is what we will be going over in the next chapter.

3

MINDFUL SPENDING

I n the previous chapter, we explored many things about banking, and you saw why holding a bank account could aid your financial goals. Our focus here is on mindful spending, and we will discuss a few prudent money management tricks you should adopt to meet your financial objectives.

I WAS TALKING about my reckless spending habit in the previous chapter; I told you how my Dad gave me an extra $10 per week for a year. I never considered that I had received $520 extra bucks from him until he summoned me into his room, wanting to know what I had done with the money I received from him over the year. I quickly told him how I had increased my daily expenses to accommodate the extra $10. I wasn't spending money wisely then; I always made sure I bought everything I wanted, even if I didn't need it.

You, too, can develop a reckless spending habit if you fail to recognize the disparity between your wants and needs.

Understanding Wants Versus Needs

Many people don't recognize a vast difference between wants and needs, so they readily spend money on their wants first. Sadly, they then end up in a terrible financial situation because they don't prioritize their needs. You can't save money or achieve your financial goals if you can't differentiate wants from needs.

NEEDS ARE NECESSITIES LIKE UTILITIES, food, healthcare, water, shelter, transportation, and medication, whereas wants are generally items that satisfy one's enjoyment or entertainment or make one's life more comfortable. Needs are crucial to one's life; wants generally... aren't. So, when it's time to spend, work on prioritizing your needs.

STILL, needs can quickly turn into wants if one isn't careful. Here are a few examples of how needs can turn to wants:

- You are purchasing coffee, bottled water, or soda instead of ordinary drinkable water.
- You are eating out instead of cooking your meals.
- You are living in an expensive home rather than a more modest apartment.

So, if there is anything you feel like purchasing, ask yourself if you can survive without it. Don't acquire something that doesn't add any value to your life.

. . .

SCHROEDER-GARDNER (2021) CAN ADVISE you how to lower your spending simply by recognizing the disparity between needs and wants:

1. Be content with what you have.

IF SOMETHING DOESN'T ADD value to your life, eliminate it. Happiness isn't measured by the things you can purchase but by the value they add to your life.

STILL, you deserve to enjoy your life and have quality time with friends and family members. So, craft a realistic budget and stick to it.

2. Don't turn needs into wants.

PAY close attention to how much you spend on your needs or risk turning them into wants. For example, you need water to stay hydrated, so don't opt for a soda, coffee, or bottled water when you can quickly get safe, drinkable water free of charge or at a cheaper rate.

3. Think before you purchase anything.

IS THERE anything you would like to purchase? Take a break and think about whether you need that item or not. Provide honest answers to these questions:

- Will this item add any value to my life?
- Why should I purchase it?
- Do I have something similar to it?

Base your purchasing decision on your answers. These questions will help you make intelligent money decisions, and you won't have to waste money on unnecessary items.

4. Evaluate your expenses.

WANTS – like the latest cellphone or a brand-new car – can drain your money. So, check where your money is going; make sure you aren't spending money on items you barely need. Trim your expenses and save more money to attain your goals.

HOW DO you prioritize wants and needs? Categorize them into high-priority needs, high-priority wants, low-priority needs, and low-priority wants. It's pretty easy to make informed purchase decisions when your needs and wants have been categorized.

SPENDING ON WANTS isn't so bad if you can be modest; just make sure you don't prioritize wants over needs. Be careful not to accumulate debt because there are certain things you have to purchase. Create a budget and stick to it.

IS THERE any advice on how I could achieve mindful spending?

Valuable Tips on Attaining Mindful Spending

Mindful spending is the attention you give to your spending habit to ensure it supports your values, needs, and financial goals. Have a deep, conscious reflection about the items you want to purchase, to see whether they can add value to your life. As I always advise, don't rush to purchase; patience is crucial to intelligent shopping. For example, why pay $100 for a gorgeous skirt which will soon be devalued to accommodate fall and winter clothes? Be patient and look for a price cut. A few days' waiting will convince you whether you need to purchase the item or not.

WALLEN (N.D.) believes that mindful spending shouldn't rob your life of the fun it deserves. He suggests that you can patiently trim your expenses a little bit to enhance saving for a vacation, college education, or possible emergencies. He hopes these tips help you spend money wisely:

1. Opt for quality.

DON'T PURCHASE a pair of shoes that could get ragged or worn out in a few weeks or months, even if they aren't expensive. For example, a $50 dress in perfect shape next year is better than a cheaper $20 outfit, which you need to change in six months.

2. Go for generic-label groceries.

.   .   .

NAME-BRAND GROCERIES COST MORE than generic-label ones. Pick a brand-name cleaning product bottle and a generic-label variant, then compare the ingredients and cost. Feel free to repeat the exercise with other products, like canned vegetables, boxes of pasta, bottled peanut butter, and medicine.

3. Reduce food wastage.

THE NATURAL RESOURCES DEFENSE CENTER study found that each American family of four wastes about 50 percent of the food they purchase (Wallen, n.d.). Isn't that a deliberate way of wasting money? Should you need to buy any food item, make sure, it is all stuff you need.

4. Exercise a bit of patience.

DON'T HURRY to make any purchase; look for rare, irresistible discounts and offers. Make sure you get your needs at affordable rates.

5. List the items to shop for.

IF YOU HOPE to avoid impulse or unnecessary purchases, create a list of the things to shop for and stick to it. Just make sure that the items you are acquiring have long-term uses and benefits.

6. Don't try to impress anyone.

. . .

YOU CAN PURCHASE anything you need, but don't spend to impress anyone. Town (n.d.) believes that many people would gladly buy brand-name clothes and fancy cars to show off or impress the people around them. If something doesn't add value to your life, it's best not to purchase it.

7. Evaluate the long-term advantages and disadvantages of your purchased items.

IT'S okay if you feel like purchasing something you admire, but discard it if the item doesn't add any value to your life. Impulse buying is something you must try to avoid at all costs.

8. Be content.

THERE CAN BE no mindful spending without contentment; be happy with what you already have. We often feel or think that we can't survive without something, but when thinking more deeply, we realize that isn't true at all. Don't spend lavishly just because you have it; instead, stay on a realistic budget when hanging out or having fun with friends and loved ones.

9. ADOPT THE "ONE-IN-ONE-OUT" method.

. . .

IF YOU BRING an item into your residence, discard any identical or similar item in the home. You could sell the lookalike item or give it to someone who truly needs it.

YOU WILL BE LESS interested in purchasing unnecessary items if you already have the ones you value and enjoy.

10. Learn to cook your foods and repair your damaged or faulty items.

YOU WILL SPEND tons of cash if you consistently eat out. Instead, cook your meals at home. Learn to repair faulty items and start making things for yourself. You shouldn't have to spend money on everything you need.

11. Attach more value to savings.

THE MONEY you save or invest usually comes with some long-term benefits. For example, you can earn interest or returns on your protected or invested capital. But any funds you use to purchase a product will be gone forever, and products will surely wear out.

12. Stick to your budget.

YOU CAN'T MODERATE your expenses if you don't work with a budget. Get rid of any spending habits which are sifting your budget. Such practices include eating out often, expensive hobbies, and overspending on clothing and other wants.

FIND a way to trim your expenses so that you can save more money. If there's a gadget you want to purchase, make sure you don't have a similar item at home; sell it if you must buy another one. Although treats might look satisfying and enjoyable, too many delicacies tend to become a lifestyle.

RECTIFY your spending habits by sticking to your budget. And, if there are any income-draining lifestyle practices in your budget, cut them. Update your financial skills if you want to cut unnecessary spending.

Vital Financial Skills Every Teen and College Student Must Have

We all have different financial goals to accomplish; while some want to purchase a house, others are eager to save up their college fees or contribute toward a retirement plan. And, since you are still in your teen years (or maybe a few years older), you have the strength to pursue, reach and attain your financial goals.

CAMPBELL (2021) SAYS that you must cultivate the following skills if you are to lose your financial objectives:

1. Access funds.

.   .   .

IF YOU HAVE A BANK ACCOUNT, learn how to deposit or withdraw money from it. Understand how to use your bank's mobile app to transfer funds, check account balance, retrieve bank statements, and run other desired operations.

2. Read a bank statement.

I'M sure you remember we talked about bank statements in the previous chapter; I told you that the report contains account balance, transactions (deposits, withdrawals, transfers), interest rates, and due dates. You must understand the content of your bank statement if you want to be successful with money.

3. Set a realistic budget.

YOU ALREADY KNOW that you can't attain a financial goal without a budget, so go ahead and create one. Use the tips provided in the previous chapter to design a reasonable budget. Just make sure your earnings exceed your expenses.

4. Distinguish needs from wants.

NEEDS AID SURVIVAL, whereas wants are mere desires of life. So, focus more on your needs if you don't want to experience a terrible financial situation. We have discussed it before, but I want to repeat it, as it is a fundamental skill and consciousness.

· · ·

5. Read and understand loan offers, credit and debit cards.

LENDERS TEND to exploit teens and young adults, who have little to no experience of how loans, credit, and debit cards function. So, you must learn to read and comprehend the terms and conditions of every financial agreement before you show your consent or approval. Should any of the terms and conditions look ambiguous, ask for clarification.

6. Get help.

YOU MAY NOT HAVE any inkling of an idea about the next financial hurdle you will have to cross. Sometimes, you need someone to guide you to make reasonable financial choices to attain your goals. What will happen if you don't know how to ask for help?

IF YOU WANT to be successful with money, you have to improve your financial skills.

DON'T HESITATE to track your daily, weekly, and monthly expenses if you hope to stay out of debt. Again, since you have already learned a few sensible money management tricks, tracing where your funds go won't be a difficult task.

YOUR KNOWLEDGE about credit and debt – our focus in the next chapter – can take you closer to or farther from your financial objectives. I hope to see you there.

4

CREDIT AND DEBT

The previous chapter tracked your daily, weekly, and monthly expenses to stay out of debt and maintain a mindful spending habit. You uncovered a few practical money management tricks you can exploit to trace where your funds go. We will focus on credit and debt in this chapter and the critical topics surrounding them.

I ALREADY TOLD you how my friends helped me raise some money during my troubling high school days. If they hadn't offered help, my indecision would have ended my academic pursuit. Indecision can cripple your finances, lower your credit score, and subject you to a lifetime of debt. The credit score of a bankrupt person is always abysmal. The score – which usually runs between 300 and 850 – defines a person's creditworthiness; a borrower with a low credit score will find it hard to get the attention of any potential lenders.

. . .

A PERSON'S credit history often determines their credit score. If you want to know your credit history, you will need to analyze your open accounts, cumulative debt, and repayment history. Potential lenders often evaluate your credit score to see whether you can repay loans within the agreed time (Kagan, 2021). Experian, Transunion, and Equifax are the primary credit reporting agencies in the United States, and they report, update and store individuals' credit histories. Although these agencies have their own varied ways of collecting data, they usually focus on the following five factors:

1. *Payment history* makes up 35 percent of the entire credit score. It indicates whether an individual pays their financial commitments on time.
2. *Credit utilization* makes up 30 percent. It is the proportion of credit a person is currently using.
3. *Duration of credit history* is 15 percent of the cumulative score. Longer credit histories are deemed safe and less risky.
4. *Types of credit* make up a 10 percent proportion. This shows a person's car and mortgage loans, credit card debts, and other credits.
5. *Inquiries on new credit accounts* point to the number of new accounts a person has and when the accounts were opened. This counts as 10 percent of the total credit score.

Your credit score can have a massive impact on your financial life. For example, you are a subprime borrower if your credit score is less than 640, and lenders would charge you higher mortgage interest than the regular mortgage interest rate. Why? Because they believe you may not pay them back within the stipulated time. Subprime mortgages also usually come with a shorter repayment period.

. . .

YOU CAN ACCESS your credit report once or twice via *www. annualcreditreport.com* for free. You've got nothing to worry about if your credit score is 700 or above; you will be able to take loans with a lower interest rate. People with impressive scores of 800 or more can easily attract potential lenders (Kagan, 2021).

HERE'S a table of credit scores and their financial status.

Credit Score	Status
800 - 850	Excellent
740 - 799	Very Good
670 - 739	Good
580 - 669	Fair
300 - 579	Poor

I'm sure that you would like to know where you stand; your initial rent or other utility deposits and the interest to pay on loans will depend on your credit score.

TO ADD TO IT, you should also know how to increase your credit score.

Creative Efforts to Improve Your Credit Score

A low credit score can negatively impact your financial goals. You need to borrow some money to augment your savings, to purchase a house or car; potential lenders won't find you credit-worthy if your credit score is poor, and you may not reach the goal.

. . .

KAGAN (2021) ADVISES that you can boost your credit score if you stick to these instructions:

1. Pay your bills on time.

PROMPTLY PAY your bills at due time for the next six months to see a noticeable improvement in your credit score. There's a penalty for anyone who fails to pay their bills by the due date.

2. Improve your credit line.

REQUEST A CREDIT INCREASE if you have two or more credit card accounts. You should get a boost in your credit limit if your different credit card accounts have good financial standings.

YOU HAVE to attain a lower credit utilization rate to improve your credit score. So, I advise you not to touch or spend the credit boost.

3. Don't close your credit card accounts.

Do you have two or more credit card accounts you aren't using? Best not to close the accounts; you will hurt your credit score if you do. Let's say that you have a $1,000 debt profile and $2,500 in each of your two credit card accounts; as it stands, you have a 20 percent credit utilization rate. Should you close one of the accounts, your credit utilization rate will turn to 40 percent, and that's going to lower your credit score.

4. Hire a credit repair agent.

IT's okay if you can't improve your credit score because of time constraints; you can pay credit repair companies to do it for you. If you must strike a deal with any of these credit repair companies, make sure they secure your financial information and records.

ARE there any logical things to learn about credit scores?

Practical Things to Know About Credit Scores and Credit Reports

If you understand these simple facts, you can improve, sustain and manage your credit scores effectively (DiGangi, 2019):

1. Credit reports versus credit scores.

A CREDIT REPORT is a detailed record of credit history, credit accounts, debt collection, and credit applications frequency. It also includes judgments, liens, bankruptcies, and other public records. A credit score may be attached to the credit report – still, they are technically different items. View the credit score as numerical analysis of the factors which make up the credit report.

. . .

SINCE YOUR CREDITWORTHINESS depends on your score, check your credit report and credit score regularly with Experian, Transunion, and Equifax (if you are in the United States) to ensure they are accurate.

2. Accessing credit scores and reports is free.

YOU DON'T HAVE to pay to get a copy of your credit report from any credit bureaus. Get a copy every four months to learn the health of your finances and catch up with any inaccuracies.

3. No penalty for checking your credit score.

HARD INQUIRIES often come with financial implications, but you've got nothing to worry about when checking your credit score. Neither does the inquiry show up on your credit report.

4. Different scoring models.

EACH CREDIT BUREAU has its scores and score ranges since they work with varying scoring models. So, ask for range clarification from your credit bureau to ascertain your current creditworthy status.

HERE'S a table on the scoring bars for major credit bureaus in the United States:

Credit Bureau	Scoring Bars
Experian	360 - 840
Equifax	280 - 850
TransUnion	300 - 850
VantageScore	501 - 990

5. Spot fraud with your credit report.

IF YOU ANALYZE your credit reports quarterly, you will likely spot any theft attempt on your identity and every financial problem. For example, if a credit card you've abandoned for some months suddenly starts spending, you can identify the issue and take appropriate action.

6. Credit scores are individual.

WHEN YOU GET married and open a joint account, perhaps you are worried that your partner's poor credit score will affect yours. The answer is it won't; credit scores are individual.

HOWEVER, moving forward, you need to be aware of the responsibility and accountability whenever you share credit because, in the end, it is still your account. If your partner fails to make the payment or sum up huge balances with your new joint account, it may affect your credit score.

7. Negative history will be wiped out.

. . .

WE ALL KNOW the importance of building and maintaining positive credit history from the get-go. However, as normal human beings, we have all made mistakes. If you have a situation in the past that has hurt your credit score, there is no need to stay down. The good news is that, as long as you start keeping and maintaining a good record, moving forward, any negative credit history in the past will eventually become less of a determining factor.

So, if you hope to build your credit score, focus more on your payment history, credit utilization, duration of credit history, types of credit, and new credit accounts.

Fundamentals of Creating a Beneficial Credit History

You may need a loan to purchase a house, buy a car, or finance education. Creditors will ask for your credit history to see whether you can manage or use credit responsibly (Take Charge America Team, n.d.). Here's how to create a positive credit history:

1. Manage your bank account well.

YOU WON'T HAVE a good credit history if you don't know how to manage your account. Try to protect the minimum balance and don't make overdrawing withdrawals.

2. Become an authorized user on a parent's card.

. . .

IT'S okay if you don't have your credit card; by becoming a legal user of your parent's card, you can use the card without having to be 100 percent responsible for it, though there could be certain limits and guidelines. Strike an agreement on the fraction of monthly card fees you will have to pay.

3. Procure a secured credit card.

THE CARD SHOULD BE TIED to your savings account, so your credit limit can't be more than your bank account's available balance. Again, linking a credit card to a savings account is great because it will help you resist the temptation of overspending since you can't spend more than your available balance.

4. Pay bills on time.

MAKE sure you pay your rent, cable, utilities, and other bills when they are due if you hope to build a desirable credit history. One missed or late payment could negatively impact your score for many years. Again, there's a penalty for every bill you neglect or forget to pay in due time.

5. Get and sustain a steady job.

SOMETIMES, your employment history can help you get a loan or lose it. No lender will lend you money if you don't have a steady job; they need assurances that you can pay it back, including the accrued interests.

WE HAVE JUST DISCUSSED the fundamentals of credit score and how it can impact your financial future. There is another thing that I believe you should be aware of at the earliest stage possible because this thing is small in size but can hugely impact your finances if you don't utilize it properly. It is called a credit card.

WHAT ARE CREDIT CARDS?

CREDIT CARDS ARE REVOLVING credits that can be used partly or in full. They have a specific credit limit and payback period. Credit cards help you obtain funds from your bank, and you will pay interest on the money.

A CREDIT CARD is simply a metal or plastic card which helps you access credit from the issuing bank; each time you use the card to purchase anything online, the card issuer shoulders the payment (Lambarena, 2021). However, it's not free money; you will have to pay it back by the month's end, including any accrued interest. Little wonder a non-specialist would say that you are spending money you don't have each time you use a credit card.

SINCE CREDIT CARDS aren't secured, no deposit or collateral is required to borrow the loan.

. . .

How Does a Credit Card Work?

YOUR BANK SETS your credit limit as soon as you are ratified for a credit card; the credit limit is the total amount the card issuer (your bank) can lend you, so use the amount at your discretion. Your income, debts, and available credit on other cards (if you have any) determine your credit limit most of the time.

CREDIT CARD TRANSACTIONS are filtered or processed by payment networks like American Express, Visa, Discover, and Mastercard (Lambarena, 2021). These payment networks ensure that funds get to the appropriate destination while the correct cardholder is equally billed. No issues if you are billed because you can pay the amount in installments or in full. Still, if you have the means, pay everything at once since partial payments accrue more interest.

I'M sure you would like to know how the credit bureaus get your payment report. Your credit card issuer mails it to them.

LET'S see the types of credit cards you can have.

Categories of Credit Cards

YOU MAY BE ISSUED any of these credit card varieties:

1. Rewards.

. . .

IF YOU ARE USING a reward credit card, you get something back each time you use it to make a purchase. Reward credit cards come in various forms:

- *Cashback cards* offer money when you make a purchase. The cash could be a bank deposit or a check.
- *Airline and hotel credit cards* provide air miles or points, which can book space in the card's partner hotel chain or airline. However, there may be particular restrictions on how to redeem rewards on these credit cards.
- *General travel cards* come with points that can be used to make travel payments. These cards are more adaptable and functional than regular airline and hotel credit cards.
- *Store credit cards* give shopping discounts, rebates, and other benefits at the card issuer's store.

Cardholders who pay their monthly bills in full love reward credit cards.

2. Low interest.

YOU DON'T GET any rewards for using a low-interest credit card; instead, you get value for your money since the card is less expensive to use. Low-interest credit cards may have a 0% A.P.R. period, so you have ample time to pay off an enormous bargain without interest. You may not be considered for such a deal if your credit score is poor.

. . .

3. Balance transfer.

USE the balance transfer credit card to push debt from another issuer when there's a lower interest rate to exploit. However, if you don't have a good or excellent credit score, you won't qualify for these cards.

4. Student cards.

BEING a college student isn't all you need to get a student credit card; under the provisions of the 2009 *Credit Card Act*, you must be 21 years or older and have proof of income before you can be issued a student credit card. Again, the applicant must also get a guarantor willing to risk their credit for them to build theirs (Lambarena, 2021).

NOW THAT WE'VE gone over credit cards, how would you go about using one?

TEENAGERS AND COLLEGE students often get excited when they hear people talk about credit cards; some see them as free money sources. I used to think that way many years ago when I was a teenager. Sure, credit cards can provide you with funds to purchase desired goods or products, but they can also cause severe financial challenges if you don't know how to use them (Muller, 2020).

. . .

You can use credit cards to enhance your credit and improve your money decisions.

Do credit cards come with any merits and demerits?

Benefits of Using a Credit Card

Using a credit card, according to Muller (2020), can help you to:

1. Organize expenses.

Credit cards make transactions convenient and straightforward. For example, you can book flights, shop online, and make other payments with your credit cards, all from a sofa in your living room.

2. Obtain cash-related rewards.

Again, some cards offer cash back, airline miles, and similar rewards to their customers.

3. Achieve convenience.

You don't have to carry cash all the time if you have a credit card. Also, with your credit card, you can run your transactions from home.

.   .   .

4. Boost security.

CREDIT CARDS ARE LINKED to banks, so they are fully secured to protect you from identity theft and fraud.

5. Improve versatility.

SEVERAL COUNTRIES USE CREDIT CARDS. Thus, travelers can always rely on them any time they move from one country to another.

STILL, credit cards have their setbacks.

DANGERS OF USING a Credit Card

COMMON DANGERS of using a credit card include:

1. Overspending.

A FRIEND once told me that money is easier spent than earned. And, since credit cards often enable you to spend money you don't have, you will overspend if you aren't reasonable with your spending.

2. Debt.

. . .

IF YOU CONTINUE to overspend money, you will accumulate debt. Credit card loans come with severe interest.

3. Awful credit history.

YOU WILL HAVE a terrible credit score if you have experienced a bad credit history. Lenders won't consider you for any significant loans or purchases if the problem persists.

Understanding Your Credit Card Statement

A credit card statement shows all your transactions with the card for a particular period; the card issuer (your bank) will send the information to you every month.

THERE IS ALWAYS a payback grace period to make partial or complete payments. Strive to pay the total amount, or be prepared to pay interest, should you carry over the balance to another month.

THERE IS some financial lingo on the credit card statement, which you need to understand to manage your accounts well. Let's take a look at the standard credit card terminologies:

1. Annual fee.

. . .

A FEE you pay for using a credit card; your bank might call it a "participation" or "membership" fee. The annual fee could be between $15 and $300, depending on the issuer.

ASK if there are banks that don't impose annual fees on their customers in your area.

2. Annual percentage rate (A.P.R.).

THIS COVERS THE PAYABLE COSTS, fees, and annual interest rate for acquiring a loan. The law requires lenders to publicize their A.P.R. Calculate the A.P.R. by multiplying the total billing periods per year with the periodic rate. For example, if you are billed four times a year, while the regular rate is 5%, the APR will be 20%.

YOU MAY HAVE different A.P.R.s listed on your credit card as balance transfers, special offers, or cash advances. If these offers have expiry dates, the balance will be added to the default A.P.R.

3. Average daily balance.

CREDIT CARD ISSUERS use the average daily balance to compute your payment due. To figure out your average daily balance, the bank adds up your daily balance and divides it by the aggregate days of a billing cycle. The bank will then multiply the average daily balance with the card's monthly periodic rate (M.P.R.).

. . .

JUST DIVIDE your A.P.R. by 12 to know your M.P.R.

4. Balance transfer.

THIS OCCURS when an unpaid credit card debt is moved to another card. Card issuers often provide extra-low teaser rates to help their customers facilitate balance transfers. Such rates or offers can be tempting, but if you can't verify when the offers will expire, don't accept them.

5. Credit limit.

THE TOTAL AMOUNT you can spend with a credit card.

6. Finance charge.

THIS COVERS interest and other charges you have to pay to use a credit card. Cash advances and balance transfers have separate finance charges. Read the lines well to identify the one you are dealing with.

7. Grace period.

. . .

CREDIT CARD DEBTS paid in full within the grace period are usually interest-free. The grace period can be 20 to 30 days after the transaction takes place.

PLEASE BE aware that some card issuers don't show such a courtesy. Cardholders with balances or debts may not be considered for the grace period.

8. Late fee.

DID YOU MISS A PAYMENT DATE? Get ready to pay the late fee. Late fees are charged monthly and could be between $30 and $35.

WHO SAYS late fees can't be eliminated in the future? Activate auto-pay on your cards if you don't want to default again.

9. Minimum payment.

LENDERS OFTEN SPECIFY a minimum amount payable to prevent your account from defaulting. The amount often approximates 2 percent of your outstanding balance.

EXCEED the minimum payment each month to reduce your credit card debts rapidly. Again, do all it takes to avoid charges.

. . .

10. Over-limit fee.

THERE IS a penalty for exceeding the credit limit of a card. The penalty is termed an "over-limit" fee. Over-limit fees can be up to $35.

YOU CAN USE your credit card wisely if you are familiar with these credit card terms.

MAKE sure that all purchase receipts are kept intact and secure; should there be any inconsistencies in your credit card statement, you will need the receipts to make necessary clarifications. Don't hesitate to put a call across to the customer care unit of your bank if there are any financial issues.

SHOULD you need help managing your credit card debt effectively, get some credit experts to counsel you.

Helpful Tips on Using Credit Cards

Credit cards can boost or hurt your credit score, but it all depends on how you use them. Still, the advantages of using a credit card will surpass its costs. Here, I will give you a few valuable tips on using a credit card:

1. Pay the balance in full.

. . .

You can evade excessive interest or finance charges if you pay your credit card debt in full during the grace period. Remember that late payments usually attract financial penalties.

Sometimes, due to unforeseen errors, you may end up paying only the minimum balance. If this continues, your debt profile will keep increasing monthly until you can't cope with it anymore. It's okay if you can't pay the whole debt at once, but try to beat the minimum payment to lessen or reduce your debt profile. Credit card issuers usually penalize cardholders who go below the minimum balance. If you can't pay the debt of a particular credit card in full, don't use the card to make payments.

2. Opt-out of pre-screened offers.

Don't open two or more credit cards at a time. Instead, focus on using just one card for your transactions. Visit *www.optout-prescreen.com* to cancel all your credit card pre-screen offers.

3. Get a reward card with a low interest rate.

Opt for a credit card with a low-interest rate, credit limit, and no annual fee. Again, it is okay if the card offers cash-back; such cards won't cause you any financial distress.

4. Set up auto-pay for your credit card bills.

. . .

AUTOMATE THE PAYMENT of your credit card debts so you don't miss them. You know you will be penalized if you fail to pay back your balances within the grace period.

5. Use only one card.

PEOPLE with multiple credit cards usually overspend. You can resist the temptation if you stick to using just one credit card.

6. Don't allow anyone to use your card.

UNDER NO CIRCUMSTANCES should you permit another person to use your credit card, especially if they won't pay you back for their purchases. Remember that you will be the one to settle the bill at the end of the month.

7. Maintain your balance.

IF YOU HOPE to keep your credit card debt under control, make sure it is less than 30 percent of your available credit.

8. Moderate your credit card applications.

. . .

IF YOU MUST MAKE another credit card application, make sure it is six months after the last one.

9. Review your account regularly.

ANALYZE your credit card account weekly to trail your spending and prevent fraud. Most credit card issuers now offer mobile apps that show all of the transactions, as well as a text notification as soon as your credit card is being used. Make sure all the transaction records are accurate. Report if you find any discrepancy.

HAVE you got any annual fee credit cards? Don't keep them active or open if you don't want to harm your credit score. You can't have healthy credit if you don't know how to use your credit card wisely.

NOW LET'S talk about something that most people think is creepy and can haunt your entire life if you don't manage it correctly. It is called *debt*.

Different Categories of Debt to Know

Each debt or loan has peculiar payment strategies, tax implications, and consequences for your credit score. Let's talk about these debt categories:

1. Credit card debt.

. . .

WE'VE ALREADY SAID a few things about this. Remember to focus on paying the debt fully within the grace period, to avoid unnecessary interest and fees.

2. Mortgages.

THESE ARE INSTALLMENT LOANS, so there's an agreed term for you to pay them back, which could be between 15 and 30 years. Since mortgages are secured loans, the purchased home automatically becomes the collateral so, should you halt payments, the lender may seize the equity and sell it to recover its money.

INTEREST RATES on mortgages are usually pegged between 3 and 5 percent. However, interest on adjustable-rate mortgages (A.R.M.) can vary yearly.

PAYMENT FOR A MORTGAGE is mainly made once each month for the term. If the property is your principal residence, your tax-deductible may be in the region of $1,000,000, whereas home equity could be up to $100,000.

PROMPT PAYMENT of mortgages can boost your credit score since it shows lenders you are a credible borrower.

3. Auto loans.

. . .

AN AUTO LOAN is quite similar to a mortgage; it is secured and has an installment payback period, usually between three and six years. Since the car serves as the collateral, the lender can seize and sell it to recover its money.

LONG-TERM AUTO LOANS usually attract lower interest rates than short-term ones. Auto loans don't have any tax implications.

4. Student loans.

THESE UNSECURED INSTALLMENT debts have flexible payback terms. Still, student loans have varied interest rates. For example, if you decide to take the loan via the United States Department of Education, the federal government will fix the rate, and it won't change before you pay it off.

MOST STUDENT LOANS have a 10-year payoff time, but there could be deviations. For example, if you can't afford your student loan, you can have a chat with your loan servicer about the need to opt for an income-based repayment plan.

WITH A GROSS INCOME of $80,000 or less, your tax-deductible student loan interest could be up to $2,500.

5. Medical debts.

. . .

LIKE STUDENT LOANS, medical debts are not secured. Again, they do not have a specific payment structure or period; each hospital or healthcare provider has its billing section. It's okay if you can't pay the entire bill at once; set up a realistic payment plan with your healthcare provider.

YOUR MEDICAL EXPENSES may be deducted from your federal taxes if they are more than 10 percent of your modified gross income.

6. Personal and payday loans.

THESE ARE cash advance debts which you may decide to pay when you get your next paycheck. Kagan (2021) affirms that these short-term loans have high-interest rates, which can go as high as 780% in annual interest rate (A.P.R.), depending on which state you are taking the loan from. A payday lender in California, for example, could ask you to pay 459% (A.P.R.) interest on a 14-day, $100 loan. Again, these loans have high finance charges because each $100 loan can attract a $15 finance fee.

I ADVISE you again to focus on paying off your debts since they can negatively impact your credit score and creditworthiness.

Potent Debt Repayment Strategies

Daly (2020) advises that you can use any of the following techniques to pay off your debts:

. . .

1. Debt snowball.

YOU ARE USING "DEBT SNOWBALL" if you always focus on using extra funds, you have to pay off your smallest debt before attending to bigger ones. Let's say you have three credit cards, which have $400, $2,000, and $5,000 worth of debt on them, respectively. After you've made the minimum payments on the three cards, you realize that you still have $150 of leftover funds, so you pay the money onto the $400 card. As soon as you clear the $400 card, you focus on the card with the $2,000 debt.

WITH THIS DEBT REPAYMENT TECHNIQUE, you can eliminate debt quickly and focus on the next one. However, more enormous debts command bigger interest rates than smaller ones, so a debt snowball may cause you savings issues since you aren't concentrating on paying off your high-interest-rate debts first.

2. Debt avalanche.

THIS IS the direct opposite of the debt snowball method: extra funds are first channeled into the highest-rate debts. As soon as a debt is paid off, attention then shifts to the next highest-rate debt.

SINCE THE HIGHEST-RATE debts command more interest, the debt avalanche method can help you save more money. Also, with this debt-repayment strategy, you can pay off a massive portion of your aggregate debt more quickly. However, more time will be required to eliminate the balances on your debt profile, which could be tough on motivation.

3. Debt consolidation.

THIS IS all about integrating several debts into one. A popular way to make this happen is by using a balance transfer credit card or personal loan to pay off all the debts.

YOU ONLY HAVE one monthly payment to make if you are using the debt consolidation technique. So, apart from making the debt repayment process more manageable, you won't have to worry about missing the due debt date. Again, with this method, you will enjoy a lower interest rate.

HOWEVER, if you don't have a good credit history, you can't opt for debt consolidation; remember that you need good credit to be considered for a debt consolidation loan or balance transfer credit card. The loan, for example, has a very reasonable interest rate.

4. Debt management plan.

A CREDIT COUNSELING agency can help you manage your debt profile for a fee. They would communicate with your creditors and arrange a debt management plan for you.

. . .

ARE you wondering if you could afford the payment plan? The agency would have a thorough financial discussion with you before it can negotiate with your creditors. As soon as the program clicks, you'll pay the agency once each month, and they'll dispense the money to your creditors. Since you make one monthly payment, this method makes debt repayment more manageable. Just be aware that credit counseling agencies will negotiate your fee waivers and monthly payment amount, but not the number of your debts.

IF I WERE YOU, I would watch these strategies closely to see how they work and select a suitable one.

Good Versus Bad Debt

It's okay for your parents or guardians always to tell you to avoid debt, but some people can't afford to purchase a home or buy a car unless they borrow money. Such loans are justifiable since they can add value to your life. Good debts might include mortgages, small business loans, and student loans.

BAD DEBTS, in contrast, won't benefit you in any way. Instead, they cause terrible financial issues (Smith, 2021). Although a reasonable debt comes with long-term benefits, a bad one doesn't have any usefulness at all. If a debt can boost your net worth and earn or make more money, the debt is a favorable one. If you borrow money to finance a project which doesn't deliver R.O.I. (returns on investment) or simply obtain a loan just for consumption, the debt is a terrible one. High-interest loans and credit card debts may constitute bad debts.

. . .

WHILE GOOD DEBTS address a person's *needs*, bad ones focus on their *wants*.

ACCORDING TO SMITH (2021), your financial situation and how much you can afford to lose often determine the status of your debts.

I'M sure that you won't have as much of a problem getting out of debt now since we've discussed some powerful debt repayment strategies you could use. If something looks blurry, reread the process to clear your doubts.

WE DISCUSSED critical topics surrounding the concepts of credit and debt management. It would be best if you got started with it. And that is what you will learn in the next chapter.

5

INVESTING

I n the previous chapter, you learned every crucial topic about credit and debt management. Here, I will expose the heart of investing, why you need to be an investor, and the appropriate steps to get started. I'm sure you will be eager to start your first investment when you finish reading this chapter. But, have a bit of patience because there are plenty of tricks to learn in the remaining three chapters.

TWELVE YEARS after we left high school in Charleston, South Carolina, I again met one of my friends. He was already a very wealthy man. I asked him how he could attain such wealth since he hadn't even turned thirty by then. He told me how he had saved $200 weekly in an investment plan for ten years and made about $140,000. He later invested that money in stocks and real estate.

HOW DID he become so rich in twelve years? I asked myself. Nothing was hidden about his upbringing: no inheritances, nor could his father afford to give him the kind of life other teenagers like him had while growing up.

YOU, too, can be successful with money if you start saving and investing. Stocks and real estate can fetch you some cool cash, but they aren't the only investment options available. Retirement plans can be wonderful avenues to grow your money and prepare for the future.

START SAVING in a retirement plan right away if you hope to attain your financial goals early in life. Just opt for a high-interest plan which could quickly grow your money. You need to start saving and investing your money because your social security benefits can't offer you a comfortable retirement.

HERE ARE some of the retirement accounts you could set up, according to Lauren Barret (2021):

- *401(k):* This is a retirement account you can open through your employer. Pre-tax payroll deductions are used to fund the account. Make sure you contribute sufficient funds to earn the full match if your employer offers any.
- *403(b):* You get to open this account through your employer if you work in a nonprofit firm or educational institution.
- *IRA:* This is an individual retirement account. You don't need your employer to open an IRA account. If you are self-employed or your employer doesn't offer a 401(k) retirement plan, the IRA can be a lifesaver.

Have you heard about the Roth IRA? It's an account you fund with after-tax money, so when you eventually want to withdraw your money, you won't pay tax on it. Roth IRA is the best way teens, and college students can save for retirement. Conventional IRAs are tax-deductible, unlike the Roth IRA accounts.

IF YOU AREN'T ready to retire, don't withdraw your IRA, 403(b), or 401(k) savings.

HOW CAN you select the right investment option to grow your wealth?

Choosing the Right Investment Option to Grow Your Money

Getting started with investing might seem risky, but you can be successful with it. Again, no matter how much you've saved, there's always a reasonable investment option you can opt for.

JUST MAKE sure you consider your income, expenses, assets, liabilities, and financial goals before you opt for any investment options. These tips can help you select suitable money-making investment options (Lam-Balfour & Royal, 2021):

1. Define your investment goals.

YOU CAN'T MAKE a perfect investment choice if you don't understand your investment goals, risk tolerance, and tools to achieve them. You can categorize your investment goals into short-term and long-term goals;

- *Long-term goals:* Retirement seems to be the universal long-term goal. A down-payment on a car, house, or college tuition may also be considered a long-term goal.
- *Short-term goals:* A Christmas piggy bank, emergency fund, or the following year's vacation qualifies as a short-term goal.

2. Identify the help you'll need.

PICK the investment option which suits your goal and channel your money into it.

SOME PEOPLE, especially first-time investors, often look for experts who can help them invest their money. If that's what you want, I have good news for you: Robo-advisors will handle your investments perfectly, at affordable rates. Robo-advisors are online investment consultants. They use advanced tech and computer algorithms to manage and grow the investment portfolios of their clients. So, you can trust them when you need automatic rebalancing, tax optimization, and human help.

3. Get an investment account.

. . .

Do you plan to purchase stocks or bonds? There's no way you can do so if you don't have an investment account. In Chapter Two, I told you that you could have a money market, certificates of deposit, and checking and savings bank accounts; similarly, there are a few investment accounts you should know about before you start investing your money.

PLEASE BE aware that some investment accounts hold tax advantages for retirement. Again, each version has its withdrawal rules. For example, you will be penalized or taxed if you withdraw your savings from your 401(k) account when you aren't due for retirement. There are other general-purpose investment accounts you could use to purchase a home, buy a car or attain any other goals. Popular investing accounts include:

- *401(k) retirement plan:* I already said a few things about this employer-sponsored investing account. So, if your employer offers the plan, embrace it.
- *Conventional or Roth IRA:* IRAs are a 401(k) lookalike; while 401(k) is provided by a person's employer, IRAs are designed for self-employed people. I already discussed IRAs at the beginning of this chapter.
- *Taxable account:* You might call this a non-retirement or non-qualified account. It's a flexible investing account that doesn't focus on any goal or objective. Since the account doesn't have any rules or specific tax advantages, you may withdraw your money anytime you want.
- *College savings accounts:* You will enjoy tax perks when you save your money in a college savings account. Notable college savings accounts include

Coverdell and 529. Contact an online broker when you are ready to open a college savings account.

4. Open the account.

SELECT YOUR ACCOUNT provider as soon as you decide the type of investment account you want to open. You have two main options;

- *Online broker:* Choose this option if you want to self-manage your account, buy and sell funds, real estate, bonds, and stocks.
- *Robo-advisor:* Hire a Robo-advisor if you are busy or don't have the required skills to manage your investments efficiently. Robo-advisors are investment experts and will charge you an annual fee, pegged at 0.25 or 0.50 percent of your R.O.I. (return on investment), to run your investments.

5. Select investments that suit your risk tolerance.

CONSIDER the amount of risk you could tolerate before choosing any investment opportunities. If you can't cope with high-risk investment options, embrace low-risk ones. Still, most times, high-risk investments yield substantial monetary returns. If you must take any risk at all, make sure it is a calculated risk.

· · ·

Here is a list of the most common investment opportunities:

- *Stocks:* These are individual company shares; stocks confer company ownership on those who purchase them. For example, if you buy shares in Coca-Cola, you automatically become part of the company's owners. The monetary value of stocks usually increases over time.
- *Bonds:* A company can issue bonds to raise funds to finance a project or debt. Since bonds are fixed-income investments, purchase them to gain regular interest payments. Bonds have fixed maturity terms, so you won't get the principal amount you invested until the bonds mature.
- *Funds:* Exchange-traded funds (E.T.F.s), mutual funds, and index funds are veritable investment options you could use to purchase bonds, stocks, and other investment items. With these funds, you can diversify your investments and boost your income.
- *Real estate:* Financial worth or value of properties continually improve from time to time. So, if bonds and stocks do not thrill you, why not consider purchasing a house?

Buying a home doesn't mean you should become a landlord. Grow your money by investing in real estate investment trusts (REIT) or any online real estate investing forum.

Does investment have any benefits?

Why Do I Need to Invest?

People used to keep all their money in a savings account or even under their beds. But, inflation can threaten the value of the money you save in those places. Invest your money in a long-term investment option like 401(k), stocks, or real estate to subdue the threat of inflation (O'Shea & Lam-Balfour, 2021).

HERE ARE the main reasons why you need to start investing your money:

1. Investing combats inflation.

THE VALUE of your money keeps improving if you invest it.

2. It improves income.

START INVESTING your money if you want to attain financial freedom.

3. It secures the future.

ONE SURE WAY TO safeguard your future is to invest in a retirement plan, like 401(k) or Roth IRA.

REINVEST your returns to make more money.

How to Invest with Little Money

Don't wait until you become super-rich before you start investing your money. Cut your expenses and invest the extra money you have left (Weliver, 2021). Here is how to get started:

1. Use the cookie jar approach.

This approach suggests that saving and investing are closely related. So, consider saving some money before you start investing it. For example, start saving $10 in a shoebox, envelope, or cookie jar weekly – if you do that consistently for a year, you will have $520.

WORK on your spending habits if you want to save more money. If you prefer online savings accounts to traditional savings tools – like a shoebox or envelope – *Chime* or *Aspiration Plus* would be perfect. If you need additional information about these online accounts, you can check their websites.

AS SOON AS YOUR "COOKIE JAR" has saved up enough money, channel it into one of the investment options you would like to invest in. You can keep repeating this as many as you like.

2. Hire a Robo-advisor.

YOU CAN STILL BE successful in investing, even if you don't have any investing experience. A Robo-advisor can help you manage your investments. Apart from their modest fees, you can start investing $500 or less if you hire a Robo-advisor.

. . .

ARE YOU A FIRST-TIME INVESTOR? I suggest you opt for *Wealth-front*. They'll charge 0.25 percent of your R.O.I. (returns on investment), but be assured that you won't pay a dime for your first $5,000; they will do it for you for free. However, you must have $500 to start investing with *Wealthfront*.

WHAT HAPPENS if you don't have up to $500? Use *M1 Finance* instead. You are good to go if you have $100, their minimum starting balance, and they won't charge you commissions or fees.

BETTERMENT IS another option you could opt for if you need a Robo-advisor. Start investing with them with $100 or less since they don't have any minimum starting balance. However, their management fee is 0.25 percent of your R.O.I.

3. Opt for brokers with a zero-percent commission.

STOCKBROKERS USED to charge a commission each time stocks were sold or bought. At the time, you couldn't venture into investing if you didn't have several thousand dollars. The whole thing has now changed, and some brokers charge little to no commission at all now. So, with as little as $1, you can start an investment.

AGAIN, you can invest your spare bucks in businesses with partial or fractional shares. So, if you don't have the funds to purchase a full share, go for a fraction of the share. Let's say you want to invest in a huge company like Apple or Google – a share of the company could be up to hundreds or even thousands of dollars. So, you can just purchase a fraction of the share if you don't have that much.

PUBLIC AND ROBINHOOD are amazing investing apps you could use as a green investor.

4. Embrace micro-investing.

I JUST SPOKE about purchasing mere fractions of shares. Yes, even those super small investments can grow your money.

LET'S say you consistently save up $50 per month and put it in your cute piggy bank. After ten years it will become $6,000. But, by investing it consistently, you will save around $8,000 (assuming a conservative 6-7% annual interest rate) – an easy $2,000 extra with the same amount of saving!

FEEL free to check and use *Acorns* to apply micro-investing of your spare money (Rapacon, 2019).

So, don't allow anything or anyone to stop you from investing your spare money. Start small and watch your investment grow. Just keep in mind a few investing rules you need to apply to attain your investment goals.

. . .

5. Enroll In a Retirement Plan

YOU CAN START by investing in your employer-sponsored plan that you can afford. You can invest as little as 2% of your salary, and you will not even notice it. Even if you are on a tight budget, this is something you can do. You can increase the contribution gradually as your salary increases or as your budget loosens up. It is a good way to start saving even with very little monthly income.

6. Start an Online Business

STARTING an online business is one of the easiest ways to make money for yourself. This is a business that is run on the internet. It is also called e-business. Starting an online business is an exciting venture. It, however, is not as easy as it might seem. One needs to be organized and determined to make it work. The online business world is pretty congested, and you need to put in the effort to set yourself apart from the rest. An online business can be selling goods online, coaching and consulting, digital marketing service, freelancing, and virtual assistant work. You can do this from the comfort of your home, and therefore very little capital is needed. This is an ideal business type for young people who are highly computer literate and want to start making money at a young age.

Investing Rules to Keep in Mind

Hey, you can't get rich or attain your financial goals if you don't start investing your money. You must choose the right investment option to grow your money or lose it. Bieber (2018) recommends that you apply these investing rules if you ever hope to attain wealth via investments:

1. Take advantage of compound interest.

I HAVE ALREADY SAID a few things about compound interest in this book. Compound interest is the act of reinvesting your investment returns to make more money. If you reinvest your returns, you can make huge money from your small and steady investments. Soon, you can attain your investment or financial goals, including financial freedom.

How? Invest in assets with reasonable return rates, though the earlier you start, the better. Such assets may include stocks, bonds, and real estate. Reinvest your investment returns into these assets and watch your money work for you.

2. Understand risks versus rewards.

EACH INVESTMENT HAS its unique risks, and high-risk investments usually have higher returns. So, evaluate the potential risks and rewards of an investment before you channel your money into it. Each person has a risk tolerance level.

YOU CAN INVEST in high-risk stocks if you want to be successful with money. Should things then go south, you should have adequate time to recover. Just make sure you don't put all of your money in a single high-risk asset, especially when you get older. Instead, identify a few low-risk investment options and diversify your investment. You will have better chances to keep your money growing positively.

3. Invest for the long-term.

YOU HAVE ALREADY LEARNED a few things about short-term and long-term investments. That's fine but concentrate on long-term investments if you hope to grow your money. And don't invest funds you'll soon need or money you can't afford to lose.

FOR EXAMPLE, you need to tie up money for several years if you invest in a retirement plan like 401(k) or Roth IRA. Early withdrawals from these accounts often come with penalties.

AGAIN, if you invest in stocks or real estate, like other assets, you may have to leave your money for many years to avoid any downturns.

4. Invest in assets you understand.

You will lose your money if you invest in assets you are unfamiliar with. So, best to take your time to research and understand the fundamentals of the investment area(s) you're yearning for. That way, you can avoid every investment disaster.

IT's okay if you want a Robo-advisor to oversee your investments for you. Robo-advisors are investment professionals, and they charge reasonable fees.

. . .

DIVERSIFY YOUR PORTFOLIO.

I'M sure you'd do everything you can to avoid significant investment losses. So, consider diversifying or spreading your investment funds across several assets, different industries, and
locations. Don't put all your money into a single investment.

YOU HAVE ALREADY SEEN the heart and soul of investing, why
you need to be an investor, that you should start early, and the
unique steps to take to get started. It's okay if you want to start
your first investment straight away, but best to create an alternative plan, so you won't suffer any setbacks if the initial plan
doesn't work. With our focus on plan Bs in the next chapter, we
will discuss the benefits of having backups to deal with unforeseen investment circumstances.

6

PLAN BS

I n the previous chapter, you saw the essence of investing, why you need to become an investor, and the creative steps to start investing your money. This chapter is strictly on the benefits of having backups and how to create alternative investment plans, to prevent any unforeseen setbacks.

I CAN TELL you that nothing is guaranteed in this life. Don't relax simply because you have a paying job already. If you fold your arms now and eventually lose your job tomorrow, how would you cope? Won't that signal the end of your unique financial goals?

IF YOU CREATE MORE income streams, you can earn more than your weekly or monthly wages and salaries, so you won't put your freedom and lifestyle at risk. Let's say you have three streams of income. For example, should one stream suffer a decline, the other two streams will generate money to pay your bills.

Exposing the Wrong Way of Creating Multiple Streams of Income

There may be some misunderstandings going around about grabbing multiple streams of income, but it's much simpler than it seems. Split your investments into different business fields to create additional sources of residual income. Simply build more streams of income to avert unnecessary risks or losses (Tressider, n.d.).

I HAVE MET people who see investment as a money game; they admire the process of building wealth because it is exciting. So, since they enjoy the game, they are eager to invest their money into stocks, bonds, real estate and other investment platforms simply because they want to create more income streams. Such people are always at risk of losing their money because they don't see investment as a challenge.

ONE WRONG WAY TO get started is to venture into several investment options at the same time. Let's say a person creates a new business, invests in stocks and purchases real estate properties within two months – the person won't be able to manage these investments and may suffer terrible losses. Reckless risk isn't a wise business strategy. You will fail if you are so irrational that you invest in business fields you know little or nothing about. It would help if you had sufficient preparation or knowledge to succeed in any business or investment.

. . .

I WOULD BE LYING if I said reckless risks don't work out sometimes. But, most times, people who take reckless risks end up disappointed. You need *calculated* risks to experience success in your investments, not reckless ones.

AGAIN, you aren't the only one trying to create additional streams of income. Your success depends on how well you can compete with other professionals trying to use the business field to improve their earnings. So, anyone who tells you that it's going to be easy is not being entirely truthful. There's always a price to pay for any additional stream of income you create.

Exploring the Proven Ways to Create Multiple Streams of Income

Here is a step-by-step process for building multiple streams of income:

1. Master your first stream.

WHAT IS your current income stream? Is it stocks, bonds, real estate or a personal business? Be deeply passionate about it. Also, try to understand it thoroughly before you start to create another one.

WHY SHOULD you master your first stream of income? Because it is where you'll learn essential investment skills and how to combat and overcome success barriers.

· · ·

2. Systemize the first stream.

CREATE a string of systems to maximize the first stream so that it doesn't require your attention all the time. You may need to hire some employees or use technology to manage the income stream. Do a few auto-pilot studies to perfect your systematizing skills.

3. Leverage your resources to build more streams of income.

USE your energy and free time to add extra income streams which could fit your skills, knowledge and network, or start from scratch with each stream.

FOR EXAMPLE, let's assume you are a marketer. You can make more money conveniently if you develop another income stream to use your current marketing skills, network and databases.

ROBERT KIYOSAKI, the author of *Rich Dad Poor Dad*, is a perfect example of someone who leveraged their resources to create extra income streams. He went into real estate and later added paper assets. He used his investment experience to create a very successful publishing business.

ARE there any income-building ideas or suggestions you could use to boost earnings?

Ideas for Additional Income Generation

It's always the case that there are additional specific financial goals to attain or more stuff to purchase; we all need money for lots of reasons. Many people say that it's easier to spend money than earn it.

I OFTEN TELL people that the problem isn't saving money but generating additional income. How can you save any if you aren't earning more than you need to run your home, especially if you are married? Elliott (n.d.) thinks people aren't making more money because they are bereft of money-making ideas.

USE any of these financial ideas to enhance your earnings:

1. Freelancing.

I KNOW someone who earns an extra $300 every week from a famous freelancing company, on top of the salary he gets from the tech firm he works with. Freelancing can fetch you some extra money, too, if you make it a side hustle. You could offer writing and coding services or work as a virtual assistant online. Freelancing offers flexible job options you can easily do from the comfort of your home. Set up a freelancing account on *Upwork, Fiverr* or *Freelancer* if you would like to earn extra money through freelancing. There are also tons of writing jobs on *ProBlogger* if you have a passion for writing.

. . .

2. Start a home-based business.

RESEARCH TO ASCERTAIN the everyday needs of people in your neighborhood, then start a home-based business that can meet those needs. Just make sure that the business excites you, or you'll soon lose enthusiasm. Again, either the business suits your existing skillset, or you learn how to do it.

FOR EXAMPLE, you can start a home-based brownie or cake business if baking thrills you. Should you crave sewing, create some gorgeous crafts during your free time – you can sell them via Etsy or Amazon.

3. Develop a course and sell it online.

CREATE an online course on any topic and sell it through *Teachable.com* – just make sure the course can add value to the lives of prospective buyers. If it does, many people will place orders, and you'll soon earn the trust of your readers or viewers (if the course is a video). *Teachable* currently sells any course which can add value to people's lives. But, based on bestseller tips, you should focus more on web-based cartoons, painting, digital scrapbooking and card magic.

THERE ARE SEVERAL ALTERNATIVE PLATFORMS, too, other than *Teachable*, which you can check out. Just use the power of *Google*, and you will instantly find out that creating and selling online courses has now become a real deal.

. . .

4. Investments.

YOU ALREADY KNOW how to run a successful investment. Bonds provide interest, while stocks yield dividends. And, if you venture into rental properties, you stand to gain rental income.

5. Peer-to-peer lending.

MANY PEOPLE ARE MAKING extra money via peer-to-peer lending outlets, like *The Lending Club*. You can also identify any of these platforms and start earning more regular bucks.

6. Social media influencer.

BEING A YOUTUBER, Blogger, or Instagrammer (not sure if that's a word), I would all put under the general category of being an influencer. If you're able to build a sizeable audience on any of these platforms, you can start to monetize your pages, whether through putting ads on your YouTube channel or blog or getting paid by brands to promote products on your Instagram feed. Being an influencer is also a great way to get tons of free stuff in exchange for promoting products/services to your audience.

SOCIAL MEDIA now can become a powerful asset, especially if you have a significant number of followers/subscribers. Any business outlets know that social media wields enormous marketing strength; you can reach out to advertisers if you can use social media to boost their sales and improve their businesses. Find a way to convince them that you can use social media to promote and enhance their business, and they will pay cool cash for you to do it.

START MARKETING your social media skills to business outfits in your local area before you start looking elsewhere.

7. Online surveys.

SURVEY JUNKIE, like other online survey platforms, can pay you when you share opinions which could help brands improve their products and services. Create a profile on their website to start taking these online surveys. You get virtual points for each survey you complete and can redeem the points via *PayPal*.

8. Affiliate marketing.

YOU ARE an affiliate marketer if you earn a commission by helping people or companies promote their products or services (Lake, 2019). Bloggers, online entrepreneurs, and anyone with a website and stable audience base can be a successful affiliate marketer.

PROSPECTIVE AFFILIATE MARKETERS should understand marketing strategies like display ads, search engine optimization (S.E.O.), content marketing, unboxing, product reviews, email marketing and paid search engine marketing (S.E.M.).

AMAZON, *ClickBank*, *Rakuten* and *ShareASale* are complex affiliate networks where you can earn lots of commissions on several products and services.

HOW CAN you become an affiliate marketer?

- Identify a company or product to promote.
- Register as an affiliate marketer to obtain a personal affiliate link.
- Add the link to your website.

If someone visits your site and clicks the link, they will be taken to the product's page to make a purchase, and you'll get a commission for each item bought via your affiliate link.

9. *Vending Machines*

I do have some personal experience in this business. When I was 13-years old, I bought my first Vending Machine. A used vending machine typically costs anywhere from $800-$3000, so it does require significant upfront investment; however, if you find the right location, they can be quite profitable for a minimal amount of effort required. Think about it; a vending machine is a perfect business. It's like running your own mini store with no employee or rent costs. A vending machine in a solid location can earn $50-$100 per week. Some of the locations you might want first to approach are factories/warehouses, hotels/inns, auto body shops, office buildings, and other high-traffic locations. You also don't necessarily need to buy the standard snack vending machine to get started. You can start small by buying a gumball machine for $200-$300 or simply by buying an honor box for $30-$70. An honor box is essentially a snack box where you leave snacks in a box and trust people to leave money in the slip of the box. You might want to place one of these in an area where people often wait, like a nail salon or a barbershop. Based on my assumptions, you can probably make $10 a week running one of these. Overall, vending machines are great businesses for young adults and teens to operate. You just need to make sure you find a good location before buying one!

PICK and utilize any of these money-making ideas and see your income grow.

OTHER THAN HAVING multiple income streams, there is something else that you should consider as plan B if something unexpected happens. It is insurance.

Efficient Insurance Options for Teens and College Students

If you hope to secure yourself, your family, and businesses or investments, purchase insurance. Should there be any illness, accident, or disaster, insurance could save you tons of dollars (Loudenback, 2019). Some say you should clock up forty or forty-five years before considering purchasing health and auto insurance policies, but life and disability insurance have nothing to do with age; I honestly think you should buy them now. Unfortunate events like accidents, disasters, and illness are common, remember. If you are hit with any of these lethal events and have no insurance to fall back on, your entire financial life will crumble. Across many U.S. states, for example, car insurance is inevitable, whereas life insurance depends on your decision.

AGAIN, insurance is relative; someone's policy type or proportion of coverage may not suit another person's financial need and situation. Also, should you have a baby or secure a new job, the scope of your insurance will change. An insurance program could be an alternative plan to prevent emergencies and save more money.

INSURANCE OPTIONS CAN INCLUDE:

1. Health insurance.

CHECK if there's any health insurance scheme in your workplace. Ask if your employer offers high-deductible health plans. You might need premium health plans to qualify for the H.S.A. (health savings account).

HOWEVER, if you have to purchase personal health insurance, check the available options to select an insurance plan you can afford. Analyze the plans offered and look at the quotes carefully from different insurance providers. Try to find the lowest rates and see if you are eligible for a subsidy based on your income. Consider using your parents' health insurance plan if you aren't quite twenty-six years old (Fontinelle, 2021). If your parents don't have a health insurance plan, opt for one which suits your income. Although some conditions can't be avoided, try to stay fit and healthy if you don't want to spend on medical bills all the time.

2. Renter's insurance.

IF YOU LIVE in a rented apartment, you have to obtain renter's insurance to protect your property from incidents like burglary or fire. Please go through the policy carefully to know the items your insurance will cover.

3. Disability insurance.

ILLNESS OR INJURY could prevent you from working to earn a living. Disability insurance can protect you from the financial agony of being unable to work. It will ensure that you keep receiving an income until you get well.

4. Auto insurance.

DRIVERS in 49 U.S. states are expected to purchase an auto insurance policy. Get auto insurance if you have or drive a car; the insurance will cover potential car damage and bodily harm caused by an accident.

IT'S hard to find a successful investor who doesn't have backup investment plans. I'm glad you've now seen the benefits of having backups and how to create alternative investment strategies to address any unexpected investment lapses.

Now you need to understand taxes inside out since returns on investment (R.O.I.) are taxed. That's exactly what you'll learn in the next chapter.

7

INCOME TAXES

I n the previous chapter, you saw the benefits of having backup investment plans and creating powerful alternative strategies to deal with unforeseen investment knocks. We will concentrate on taxes here, and I will tell you the fundamentals you need to know.

PAYMENT OF TAXES isn't a choice; it is obligatory for people who are earning money. You must understand how income is taxed, even if you have yet to receive your first paycheck. Let's assume a company offers you a $2,500 salary per month. Calculate the after-tax value of the salary to see if it could sustain and assist you in achieving your financial goals and obligations. PaycheckCity.com, like many other online calculators, can be used to estimate your after-tax salary.

AGAIN, remember that income taxes are due as soon as you are paid and may be deducted from your paychecks. So, if you just got your first job, congratulations. You may still be living with

Dad and Mom, but since you now have a job, you will be paying various taxes, like every other American, if you live in the U.S. (Aspiriant Fathom, 2017).

Do You Need to File Taxes?

First, you need to figure them out based on your marital status and annual gross income. Here is the latest standard deduction for the 2020-2021 tax year (*Nerdwallet*, 2021):

Filing status	2020 tax year	2021 tax year
Single	$12,400	$12,550
Married, filing jointly	$24,800	$25,100
Married, filing separately	$12,400	$12,550
Head of household	$18,650	$18,800

So, for example, if you are single and your current monthly salary is $1,000, which will bring you an annual of $12,000, it means you don't have an obligation to file your taxes because your annual gross income will be less than $12,400. But, let's say you get a raise to $1,500/month – which will bring your annual income to $18,000 – then $18,000 - $12,400 = *$5,600*, which will be taxable, and you have to file for it.

HOWEVER, even if you don't need to file taxes, you may still want to do so. If your employer withholds taxes from your paychecks, or you qualify for earned income tax credit (E.I.T.C.), you can get a refund, even if your earning is less than the filing requirement.

LEARNING How to File Your Taxes

. . .

YOU COULD USE an online program or tax software to file your taxes. But, if you don't feel like doing it yourself, hire a certified public accountant or a tax preparer. Lest you forget, you will need the *1040EZ* tax form, employer-generated *W-2*, income stubs, and *1099-MISC* to file your taxes.

LET'S say your modified total income stands at $72,000 or less; you won't pay a dime to file your federal income taxes using the *I.R.S. Free File*. *TurboTax*, like many online tax preparation companies, offers free tax-filing services in partnership with the I.R.S. People with a 1040 return or who aren't qualified for itemized deductions can use *TurboTax* free tax-filing services.

JUST BE aware that April 15 is the due date for taxes, though you should check the I.R.S. website to know the deadlines for different tax filing methods. File your taxes early if you hope to get your refund soon; you might lose your refund to an identity thief if you delay the process. Also, run the filing procedure electronically to have the rebate quickly deposited into your bank account.

USE a check to pay your taxes, or simply run the payment directly from your bank account, debit, or credit card. No problem if you can't pay the entire tax bill by the due date; talk to the I.R.S. to see if you can reach an installment agreement with them.

THERE ARE a few effortless tax-filing things you can learn to run the process efficiently.

Helpful Tips About Filing Taxes

Remember that your annual tax return must be filed with the I.R.S. on April 15 or earlier! And, since you may have to do it personally, I advise you to keep a thorough record of your income and expenses. Be organized and start working on your earnings and expenditures. With that, you won't have any issues creating a detailed record of your income and expenses. Essential things to deal with include:

1. Pay as you go.

HAVE YOU HEARD OF "PAYCHECK SHOCK"? If this is your first job, you probably haven't. By the time your first paycheck is issued, you will know what paycheck shock means. But I won't let you wait until then. Paycheck shock occurs when you suddenly realize that the amount paid into your account is lower than the salary you bargained with your employer.

THE LAW COMPELS your employer to deduct state and federal taxes from your salary, including Medicare and social security funds. You likely filled the *W-4* form before starting your current job and stated some allowances there. The amount you pay to the I.R.S. and state tax agencies depends on what is said in the form. So, after your taxes and other funds have been removed, your take-home could be 20 or 30 per cent lower than your cumulative income.

2. Tax returns.

. . .

You need to file your annual tax return to avoid any horrible, income-shrinking tax deductions. Tax regulations could be time-consuming and complicated. Still, you won't have to struggle to file your tax if you understand the process.

Always remember that your income taxes run through January 1 and December 31 without breaking. Your employer(s) should send you *Form W-2* and the previous year's cumulative earnings, paid taxes, and other contributions. Your bank will also send you your earning and interest updates. Since you may need your annual tax records to correct possible figure disparities, I suggest keeping them secure.

Get ready to file a federal tax return if you are single and don't hang on anyone's tax return, especially if your annual income is up to $10,350. If you can find someone who would claim you as a dependent, it is best to do so. Then, if any of these situations apply to you, file the tax return:

- You earned over $6,300.
- You have over $1,050 unearned income, like interest or dividends.
- Your total income is up to $6,310 or more.

Check whether your state has a different tax requirement.

My advice is to keep your tax receipts in a secure place.

Vital Things to Know About Taxes

Tax day pops up only once a year, yet keeping up a stunning tax profile can feel like a year-long task. You could file your tax or hire a tax professional to do it, but you might end up with a few money issues if you don't understand specific filing obligations (Erb, 2016). Here are crucial things you must know about taxes:

1. A federal income tax return isn't for everyone.

SOME PEOPLE ARE exempt from filing a federal income tax return, even if they earned income during the calendar year. For example, your filing status, age, the amount earned, and the source of the revenue determine whether you should file the tax return or not. For more information or clarification, visit the I.R.S. website.

2. Enjoy tax breaks and credits if you can't file a federal income tax return.

SINCE TAX CREDITS are dollar-for-dollar reductions in tax due, they offer more financial benefits than tax deductions, which only reduce a person's taxable income.

EVEN WHEN YOU owe no tax, the American Opportunity Credit (A.O.C.) may send you money in the form of credits. Tuition and fees fall under A.O.C. qualified expenses for students. The maximum credit for each eligible student is $2,500, and 40 per cent of this fund may be refundable.

. . .

WORKING people and those with moderate income could opt for the earned income tax credit (E.I.T.C.). Some people erroneously assume that you must have kids before being considered for the E.I.T.C., but having kids may only boost or improve the benefit. Although people without qualifying kids could access credits to the tune of $503, those with three or more kids could achieve up to $6,242.

3. Certain deductions don't require itemization.

IT WOULD BE best to itemize to enjoy most deductions, so they miss out automatically since most taxpayers don't itemize. Yet, all isn't lost since the I.R.S. has a few deductions you can enjoy without itemization. Just grab *Form 1040* and check its front page to see these deductions. Some of the deductions include moving expenses, IRA, and student loan interest.

4. Make estimated payments if you are self-employed.

WE USE A PAY-AS-YOU-GO TAX SYSTEM. That's why your employer withholds taxes from an employee's paycheck and transfers the same to the I.R.S. (Internal Revenue Service). So, the employee may owe taxes, break-even, or be owed by the I.R.S. at the close of the year.

SELF-EMPLOYED FREELANCERS, landlords, shareholders, and everyone with *Form 1099* can make estimated payments. Such people can download *Form 1040ES* from the I.R.S. website and use it to make their estimated payments.

PAY your estimated taxes quarterly if you fall under this category. Should you pay late or skip a payment, get ready to pay a penalty fee.

5. File a return when you can't pay off your tax bill.

IF YOU FAIL to pay your tax bill or file a return, you will be penalized. Still, you can avoid one of these penalties and lessen the financial mess on your wallet. Don't empty too much if you can't pay off your tax bill on tax day; there are a few payment plans or arrangements you can make with the I.R.S. if you don't want to pay with your credit card all at once.

6. Due dates matter.

MAKE sure you file your returns and pay your tax bills by due dates to avoid interest and penalties, which could pile up quickly. Ask for an extension if you believe you can't file your returns or pay your tax bills by their due dates.

7. An extension of time to pay tax bills is different from an extension of time to file returns.

·   ·   ·

I ALREADY SAID you could ask for an extension of time if you believe you can't file your tax return when it's due; use *Form 4868* to request an extension. Extension of time comes with no cost if you don't owe any tax bills. But, should it go the other way, you would have to make payment to avert penalty and interest.

Understanding the Process of Tax Computation

Tax owed depends on the income you generate.

THERE ARE two forms of income: earned and unearned. Earned income covers earnings on paid jobs and may include salaries, wages, tips, and commissions. Unearned income isn't the direct gain of your weekly or monthly efforts. Most times, it comes from your investment, technically called R.O.I. (returns on investment). Such returns usually come in the form of capital gains, interest, or dividends.

ALTHOUGH YOU MAY ONLY HAVE to pay income taxes for your unearned income, you could be subjected to income and payroll taxes for your earned income. Gifts, life insurance proceeds, child support, after-tax premiums on disabilities, and inheritance are not taxable.

THE I.R.S. USES a cycle of ranges (also called "brackets") to depict or represent your incremental income. Then, they will evaluate your modified gross income (after they've made some deductions from your cumulative income). Qualified moving expenses, alimony, and IRA contributions are some of these deductions.

. . .

TAX DEDUCTIONS WILL REDUCE your earnings a little bit. However, you can claim a standard or itemized deduction. The standard deduction is a fixed amount based on your filing status, whereas itemized cover the deductions which may apply to you. Itemized deductions include property taxes, medical and education expenses, charitable contributions, and mortgage loan interest. Opt for standard deduction if you have a straightforward financial situation. But, should you be someone who gives a lot of money to charity, pays income taxes, extensive medical bills, or runs several investments, choose the itemized option.

LEGITIMATE ITEMIZED DEDUCTIONS INCLUDE:

- Property taxes, like state income or sales taxes.
- Health-related expenses greater than 10 percent of your A.G.I. (or 7.5 percent if you are 65 years or older).
- Mortgage interest on residences to the tune of $1 million and interest on residence equity loans up to $100,000.
- Generous donations to tax-exempt institutions.
- Margin interest and other investment interest expenses.

Other things you could itemize are:

- Employer-withheld expenses, like professional dues, uniforms, and unreimbursed travel expenses.
- Investment advisor fees.
- Tax-preparation fees.

However, these additional expenses must exceed 2 percent of your A.G.I. before you can itemize them.

REMEMBER that you can't deduct credit card interest, political contributions, or loan interest on a private car.

STILL, you could claim a personal exemption for yourself, your spouse, and your qualified dependents. The exemption is the amount you could deduct from your adjusted gross income (A.G.I.). The amount was $3,950 as of 2014. There are three categories of personal exemptions that you could claim:

1. Yourself.

EACH PERSON CAN CLAIM one exemption for themselves.

2. Your spouse.

A JOINT RETURN could be filed by married couples: one for the husband and the other for the spouse.

3. Dependents.

PEOPLE with qualified dependents can file an exemption for each of them. A dependent could be one's child or relative.

. . .

WHAT MAKES ONE A QUALIFIED DEPENDENT?

A CHILD'S AGE, residency, relationship with you, and means of support can make them eligible. Again, apart from your relationship with a relative, their qualification depends on their gross income and the amount of support you can give them. Should you need further clarification on this, visit the I.R.S. website *www.IRS.gov*.

CALCULATE your tax due and taxable income as soon as you know your A.G.I., deductions, and exemptions. A comprehensive tax table and advice on taxable and non-taxable income are readily available on the I.R.S. website; again, the tax due depends on your tax rate. Should you need to estimate the amount you owe or refund you should get, subtract your payment (tax credits) from your tax due.

BE aware that your A.G.I. is a vital fraction of your tax calculation. To calculate the A.G.I., certain deductions need to be made from your cumulative income. These deductions, according to Schwab (n.d.), include:

- Deductible IRA contributions.
- Alimony.
- Contributions to a self-employed retirement plan.
- Penalty on early withdrawal of savings.
- Teacher education expenses, to the tune of $250.
- Qualified education interest.
- Qualified higher-education expenses.
- Half of self-employment taxes.
- Self-employed health insurance.

- Qualified moving expenses.

Why is the A.G.I. so important?

YOUR ELIGIBILITY for certain credits and deductions depends on your A.G.I. For example, if your A.G.I. is more than $114,000 or $191,000, you can't contribute to a Roth IRA as a single or married tax filer, respectively.

Clarifying the Truth About Tax Rate

The tax rate covers the percentage of income you pay in taxes; the amount depends on the size of your income. There are two significant types of tax rate:

1. Marginal tax rate.

THIS IS the ratio or proportion of tax paid on the last dollar of your taxable income. In other words, your marginal tax rate is the additional tax paid on each extra dollar you earn.

2. Average tax rate.

THIS IS the regular tax you often pay. Divide the total tax paid by your total earnings to calculate your average tax rate.

. . .

FOR EXAMPLE, John is single, and his taxable income stands at $40,000. His marginal income tax rate would be 25 percent, whereas his average tax rate could be a bit lower.

LET'S say you want to quit your current job because you desperately need a salary increase. Asking for a raise isn't a bad thing, but you must first consider the impact of your marginal tax on the raise. For example, if your marginal tax rate is 10 percent, 10 cents of the extra dollar you earn will be used to pay tax. So, you may not be getting the raise you so desire.

HERE'S a table on the U.S. statutory marginal tax rates:

Rate	For Unmarried Individuals	For Married Individuals Filing Joint Returns	For Heads of Households
10%	$0 to $9,950	$0 to $19,900	$0 to $14,200
12%	$9,951 to $40,525	$19,901 to $81,050	$14,201 to $54,200
22%	$40,526 to $86,375	$81,051 to $172,750	$54,201 to $86,350
24%	$86,376 to $164,925	$172,751 to $329,850	$86,351 to $164,900
32%	$164,926 to $209,425	$329,851 to $418,850	$164,901 to $209,400
35%	$209,426 to $523,600	$418,851 to $628,300	$209,401 to $523,600
37%	$523,601 or more	$628,301 or more	$523,601 or more

Source: Tax Basics

THERE'S another tax rate you must know about if you hope to be successful with money. It's called the "combined marginal tax rate," capturing federal and state income tax rates. For example, if your federal and state taxes are 25 and 5 percent, respectively, your combined tax rate will be 30 percent of your taxable income. You can't get the actual value of your R.O.I. if you aren't familiar with this tax rate.

Using Tax Credit

Use a tax credit to reduce your taxes, dollar for dollar. The tax credit doesn't just lower your taxable income like a deduction. It ensures that the reduction reflects on the amount of taxes you'll pay. For example, a $100 credit automatically lessens your taxes by $100 (Schwab, n.d.).

DEDUCTIONS, as you already know, are removed from a person's income to lower their taxes. Tax credits reduce the tax amount a person owes. You may still owe some tax amounts after you've claimed all deductions available. However, you can use tax credits to lessen your tax debt or erase it (Schreier, 2021). Tax credits come in three major types: nonrefundable, refundable, and partially refundable.

NONREFUNDABLE TAX CREDITS can only be used in the current reporting year; you can't carry them over to the coming years. Although a nonrefundable tax credit may be used to lessen or lower tax liability to zero, you can't use it to get a tax refund. Nonrefundable tax credits include mortgage interest credit, lifetime learning credit, credits for adoption, and dependent care credit.

REFUNDABLE TAX CREDITS offer taxpayers the entire amount of the credit. For example, each taxpayer will get a refund for the credit if the refundable tax credit decreases their tax liability to zero. Earned income tax credit and the premium tax credit are examples of refundable tax credits.

IT's a little different with a partially refundable tax credit. For example, if your tax liability is zero before using the total amount of a tax credit, the remainder credit may be refunded. The American education tax credit is an excellent example of a partially refundable tax credit.

TAX CREDITS COME in different forms, so opt for the one which suits your income and personal situation. Available tax credit options include:

- Qualified adoption expenses.
- A qualified child under 17.
- Child and dependent care credit.
- Residential energy.
- The American education tax credit, for the first four college years' qualified expenses (once known as the "Hope Credit").
- The lifetime learning credit, for improving job-related, skill-enhancing expenses and undergraduate, graduate or professional degree attainment.
- A premium tax credit, used when purchasing health insurance for individuals and families.
- The earned income tax credit, for low-income individuals and families.

Earned income tax credit is quite different from other tax credits already mentioned; it only offers a refund, not a credit against taxes due. Visit the I.R.S. website to learn more about it.

. . .

Learning Everything About Tax Refunds

The I.R.S. pays a lot of tax refunds every year. Still, many teens and college students know little to nothing about these refunds.

A tax refund is a repayment to a taxpayer who overpaid their taxes to a state or federal government (*Tax Refund*, 2021). Many taxpayers often see a refund as free or bonus money, but that's not the truth; it's nothing but an interest-free loan a taxpayer gives to the government.

Interest-free loans, like tax refunds, may negatively impact your finances, but you can avoid them. How? Get to know why you overpaid your taxes and prevent possible recurrences. Here are the likely causes of overpaid federal or state taxes:

1. The taxpayer didn't fill their I.R.S. *Form W-4* correctly.
2. The taxpayer didn't update the form to indicate they have a child and are entitled to a child tax credit.
3. The taxpayer deliberately manipulated *Form W-4* to generate an enormous tax refund.

So, the refund you get depends on what's being withheld from your paycheck. Still, if what's removed is too little, you'll be charged an underpayment penalty. U.S. savings bonds, personal checks and direct deposits may be used to issue your tax refunds.

. . .

REFUNDS ARE FASCINATING, but you gain more if you don't overpay your taxes. Refunds are interest-free loans, remember.

Understanding Payroll Taxes

A payroll tax is a proportion of an employee's paycheck, which is withheld by the employer and sent to the government through the I.R.S. The tax may be deducted from employees' wages, tips, and salaries (Kagan, 2021).

FOR EXAMPLE, in the United States, federal payroll taxes are mainly used to finance Medicare, workers' compensation, and social security programs. So, these taxes are often tagged as FICA or MedFICA on pay stubs.

WAGE or salaried employees should know that they won't shoulder the entire payroll tax; payroll taxes are usually split into two equal sums: the employer settles a fraction, while the other part is withheld from each employee's paycheck. Self-employed people have to pay the full amount.

CERTAIN PAYROLL TAXES have yearly limits. For example, if your income is more than the social security wage base, you won't have to pay the social security tax in the United States. As of 2021, the wage base is pegged at $142,800.

SOCIAL SECURITY HAS A SALARY LIMIT, but Medicare has none. For example, a 6.2 percent social security deduction applies for a maximum salary of $142,800. Indeed, Medicare doesn't have any salary restrictions, but you will pay 0.9 percent for

Medicare if your income is $200,000 or more (apart from 2.9 percent for Medicare).

FREELANCE WRITERS, musicians, contractors, small-scale business owners, and other self-employed people need to pay their payroll taxes, also known as self-employment taxes. The self-employment tax rate is 15.3 percent and covers social security (12.4 percent) and Medicare (2.9 percent). But, don't forget, you'll pay an extra 0.9 percent of your self-employment earnings on $200,000 or more.

PERHAPS YOU NEED to open a tax-advantaged account to lower your taxes.

Uncovering Tax-Advantaged Accounts

A tax-advantaged account means a tax-deferred or tax-exempt investment, financial, or savings plan. Such accounts come with a few tax benefits and may include partnerships, U.I.T.s, municipal bonds, and annuities, as well as IRAs, 401(k), 403(b), and similar retirement plans (Chen, 2021).

MANY INVESTORS and employees use tax-advantaged accounts to improve their financial situations. For example, employees use Roth IRA, 403(b), 401(k), and employer-sponsored retirement plans to secure their future, even as each high-income taxpayer is eager to embrace the tax-free, municipal-bond income.

. . .

TAX-EXEMPT AND TAX-DEFERRED statuses remain the standard methods people use to reduce their tax bills. Decide which methods (or both) to use to enhance your finances. after you've analyzed the timeframe to get their benefits.

- *Tax-deferred accounts:* You will get immediate tax deductions on the entire amount deposited in a tax-deferred account. However, you will be taxed for successive withdrawals. Conventional IRAs and 401(k) plans are popular tax-deferred retirement accounts in the United States; as suggested by the account's name, taxes on income are delayed or deferred. Let's say $40,000 is your taxable income this year, and you saved $3,000 in a tax-deferred account. This means you only paid tax on the remaining $37,000. Perhaps you adopted the saving strategy for the next thirty years or until you retire. Any withdrawals you make will reflect on your taxable income: for example, if you withdraw $4,000 from the tax-deferred account, your taxable income will jump from $40,000 to $44,000, which means you would start paying the taxes you've been delaying for the past thirty years.
- *Tax-exempt accounts:* A tax-exempt account offers several future tax benefits, including future tax-free withdrawals. Since contributions are after-tax dollars, tax-exempt accounts have no immediate tax advantage. Investment returns in a tax-exempt account are tax-free.

Roth 401(k) and Roth IRA are prominent tax-exempt accounts in the United States. So, if you put $1,000 in a tax-exempt account and invest the funds in a 3-percent annual-return mutual fund for thirty years, the account will make an extra $1,427 (excluding the initial $1,000 deposit); the $1,427 won't be taxed.

WHILE TAXES for a tax-exempt account are paid now, those for a tax-deferred account are paid later.

Tax Records to Keep

Don't discard any financial records, including your tax documents, because you might need them. Taxpayers should secure their tax returns for at least seven years. Should there be any disparity in your tax records, you will need your tax statements to reconcile or harmonize your tax accounts.

TAX ITEMS TO PROTECT INCLUDE:

1. Documents that clarify your income and deductions- Such documents include receipts for generous contributions, W-2, 1099s, and canceled checks.
2. Papers which highlight home improvements and ownership statements. Be aware that you will need these documents to compute your tax basis if you have to sell your property in the near future.
3. Records of your investments, especially those indicating the items you either purchased or sold.
4. Statements for your retirement accounts and after-tax contributions

Secure these documents if you hope to avoid tax-related financial problems in the future.

. . .

WE UNCOVERED everything you need to know about federal and state taxes in this chapter. Going forward, I'm sure you won't have any problems managing your taxes.

IN THE NEXT CHAPTER, you will learn vital tips to make significant decisions later in your life. Hope to see you there.

8

"ADULTING" DECISIONS

In the previous chapter, we analyzed federal and state taxes, and you learned how to manage your taxes. Great! This chapter will lead you toward making crucial decisions to improve your finances and increase your money.

I WAS a sweet sixteen when I first nursed the idea of owning a home. I told myself I could achieve the dream before marking my 24th birthday if I started saving from now. Indeed, that was a very optimistic goal, but it was possible. That time, I already had four different, regular freelance jobs, which were fetching me a few extra bucks per week. And, if the money I saved wouldn't be enough, I would take a loan to attain the objective.

I FELT I should let Dad know what I intended to achieve in the next eight years. He said: "Son, owning a house breeds so much satisfaction and happiness, but the extra costs of maintaining a home can endanger your finances, so don't rush it." I told myself that I wouldn't rush it and finally bought a house when I turned thirty. You may hurt your finances if you rush to purchase a home.

Should **You Rent or Purchase a House?**

If you feel like buying a home after seeing your friends purchase theirs, that's totally normal. I will encourage you to do so if you can afford it. But, if you can't, consider renting an apartment. Buying a house when you aren't ready for it can cause you several financial problems.

How will you know when you're ready to purchase a house? Provide honest answers to these questions:

1. Have you settled your student loans and other debts?
2. Have you saved a full emergency fund?
3. Can you raise a 10 or 20 percent down-payment for a 15-year, fixed-rate mortgage?
4. Is the house payment 25 percent (or less) of your monthly salary?
5. Will you live in the location for the next five years or more?

Go ahead to purchase a house if your answer to all of these questions is *yes*. Should you say no to any of the questions, I suggest focusing on improving your earnings and growing your money first.

Pros and Cons of Purchasing a House

. . .

EVEN IF YOU said yes to all of the questions above, you must make sure that you *want* to purchase. I'm sure you'll make the right decision after you've seen the pros and cons of purchasing a home:

PROS:

1. Each payment brings you closer to being a homeowner.
2. The home's value will improve over time, and you may cash it in at any time. For example, the house you purchased for $250,000 today could sell for $330,000 in the next two or three years.
3. You tend to enjoy several tax benefits. For example, you could list your mortgage interest as a deduction on your tax return.
4. You are free to renovate the house, change the paint or do anything you like with it.
5. You can enjoy more privacy, security, and peace of mind.

Cons:

1. You can't travel or relocate quickly since selling a house at the desired price might be difficult.
2. You'll have more financial responsibilities and expenses to settle. These expenses include homeowner's insurance, homeowners' Association (H.O.A.) fees, utility bills, flood policy, and property taxes.
3. The home value may start to decline. For example,

the pipe could leak, and you would have to get it fixed.

Pros and Cons of Renting a House

HERE ARE the pros and cons of renting a house:

PROS:

1. You can travel or move from one city to another.
2. You don't need to worry about any instability of housing expenses.
3. The landlord will shoulder the cost of house maintenance.

Cons:

1. Rent could increase yearly.
2. You can't enjoy tax deductions, property value, or financial incentives.
3. You can't customize your space without the landlord's express permission.
4. The landlord may terminate your tenancy or sell the house.

Analyze the pros and cons of purchasing or renting a house before you make your housing decision.

Top Housing Tips for Teens and college students

It would be best if you only decided to rent or purchase a house after you've been through the pros and cons above. Should you have any issues arriving at a decision, these tips can bridge the gap:

1. How long do you intend to stay in the house?

PURCHASE a home if you'd like to live there for five or more years. Consider renting an apartment if you think you'll be leaving the house soon or traveling frequently.

2. Will your current life situation change soon?

YOUR HOUSING NEEDS depend on your situation; don't purchase a house if your status might change in the next three or four years.

3. What can you afford?

REMEMBER that you must create a budget and stick to it. Renting a house isn't as expensive as purchasing one; you have to pay so many upfront costs when you buy a home. So, don't buy a house you can't maintain.

YOU CAN SAVE up some money to purchase a house while you're living in a rented apartment.

·   ·   ·

4. Have you weighed the pros and cons of renting or buying a house?

RENT an apartment if you won't be staying in the area for more than four or five years, especially when you aren't ready to become a homeowner yet.

STILL, if you have the money and believe it's time you had your own house, you can make a purchase. Just make sure the price is reasonable.

Efficient Steps on Purchasing Your First Home

Buying a home is deemed a massive financial goal or landmark in life since it requires a considerable commitment. Preparation is crucial if you hope to attain the goal soon (Caldwell, 2020). A first-time homebuyer can enjoy many financial benefits, like tax breaks and access to state programs or federally backed loans; these benefits can lower their down-payments.

SHOULD you decide to buy a home, take these simple steps:

1. Determine your level of readiness.

OWNING a house can be very expensive. Again, it comes with extra costs like electricity, home repairs, garbage pickup, utility fees, taxes, and insurance. These costs can threaten your finances if you aren't ready for them. Consider your budget and savings to see how much you could put on a mortgage payment.

Check if you have sufficient money for the down-payment and closing costs. It's okay if you hope to get a loan, but it will interest you to know that lenders usually restrict house expenses to 30 percent of borrowers' monthly gross income. So, it would be best to check your credit to see if you've any chance of qualifying for a loan.

2. Consider the type of home.

THERE ARE many home options to choose from. While some crave a multi-family building housing two to four units, others prefer a simple, conventional, single-family home. Other alternatives include a condo, duplex, and townhouse. Just make sure the home you are purchasing has the specific features and conveniences you admire. Does the house meet your size, neighborhood, and layout specifications?

3. Reduce or pay off your debt.

FIND a way to reduce your debt or pay it off before purchasing a house. You should also improve your emergency fund if you hope to cope with the extra costs of owning a home. You will not be ready to own a cottage yet if you still have a bunch of high-interest credit card debt to service or pay off.

4. Shop for a loan.

. . .

SOMETIMES YOU NEED a loan to acquire or purchase a house. So, I would say you should get pre-approved for a mortgage before looking for a residence to purchase. The pre-approval can give you an idea of the amount you can afford.

USE a mortgage broker if you want additional options. Since the broker can show you many loan companies and programs, you can easily choose the best rates.

5. Uncover the best loan types and payment options.

OPT FOR A 15, 20, or 30-year mortgage loan since they will have a lower monthly payment.

MORTGAGES CAN HAVE adjustable or fixed payment rates. While market conditions usually fluctuate the adjustable rate, a fixed-rate mortgage isn't affected by economic or market instabilities; stability in monthly payment can be attained if you choose the fixed-rate mortgage – but, should rates fall, you'll miss out.

6. Be pre-approved.

DON'T PLACE an offer on a house if you haven't been pre-approved for a loan. Why? Because no seller will entertain an offer that doesn't come with a mortgage pre-approval. So, apply for a mortgage and complete the paperwork to get the pre-approval.

. . .

7. *Prepare a down payment.*

A DOWN PAYMENT can reduce your costs. For example, you can get private mortgage insurance (P.M.I.) if you make a down-payment of 20 percent of the actual price of the home. Success in homeownership doesn't depend on the 20 percent down-payment, but you must evaluate the cost of P.M.I. suppose you're purchasing a residence. Review the rates of major online mortgage lenders to get the most affordable one.

8. *Get an experienced real estate agent.*

FIND the agent once you are pre-approved for a mortgage and have decided the amount you can afford. After listening to your needs and wants, the real estate agent should explain the market and identify a home that suits your budget and needs. The real estate agent should help you negotiate the terms and counsel you through the paperwork until the deal is completed.

9. *Inspect the home.*

CAREFULLY INSPECT the home to ensure that it has all the conveniences and features you want. The home inspection isn't a home appraisal; consider hiring an independent home inspector to do the task. A home inspector will check the home to see any issues or hidden problems; from the inspection, you will know if the house has termites, mold, or foundation problems, or whether there's a roof you need to replace. The findings should guide you during negotiations.

. . .

10. Be patient during escrow.

PREPARE to go through the escrow phase once the bid and offer have been accepted. The escrow ensures that documents, money, and other vital information are prepared and processed and can offer sufficient protection to the buyer, seller, and lender.

THE ESCROW STAGE could take up to three to five weeks, depending on the factors which need to be considered.

11. Close and move in.

SIGN the decisive papers once it is the closing date. The escrow agent will make sure the funds get to the appropriate parties.

ENJOY YOUR HOME, but don't forget to visit your bank to update your address. Consider setting up your utilities and discontinuing the old ones to save money and avoid late fees.

Dealing with a Car Purchase

Each person has their own relative thoughts about cars; while some fancy the latest arrivals, others fear new cars. It's pretty easy to purchase a new car nowadays, all thanks to no-down-payment offers and low-interest auto loans (Mercadante, 2019). You have to ask yourself if you honestly need a car.

· · ·

LET'S say you already have a car. For example, if the vehicle needs regular repairs and maintenance, you will struggle to cope with the repair bills. Buying a new car could then be a reasonable action. If your current vehicle no longer suits your lifestyle or family size, buy another one.

STILL, consider the financial implications of a new vehicle on your finances. A new car can be costly; it can drain your savings and subject you to hardship and debt.

ANALYZE these factors before sanctioning your decision to buy a new car:

1. Repair bills on the current car.

ANY VEHICLE, new or old, must be maintained from time to time. An ageing car may require endless and costly repairs, and this could weaken your finances.

LET'S say you need to pay $400 monthly to acquire a new car; you will have paid $4,800 in twelve months. Compare this amount to your car's annual repair expenses to make an informed decision. For example, if you have three repairs per year on your vehicle at $1,500, don't purchase a new one yet. But, should you spend $3,500 for five or six repairs a year, get a new car.

· · ·

2. Too much downtime.

IF YOUR CURRENT car breaks down often and takes tons of money or time to be fixed, consider getting a new one; you might not want to go carless or depend on other drivers and rental cars all the time.

FOR EXAMPLE, you might spend only $1,500 to repair your ten-year-old vehicle. That's inexpensive, isn't it? Still, if the car had eight or nine breakdowns in a year, and you had to go carless for thirty days, you might then decide that keeping the auto makes no sense. Dependability and costs can determine if you should keep your old car or purchase a new one.

3. Revamped equipment.

TODAY'S AUTOS are so reliable that you can ride the same car for ten or fifteen years, all thanks to improvements in technology. But, you might not get the equipment you admire in an aged vehicle. For example, suppose your old car doesn't have safety features like anti-lock brakes, forward collision warning capability, and airbags. In that case, you may decide to purchase a new one, especially if you have kids to protect.

4. Doesn't fit your lifestyle.

A CHANGE in your lifestyle can affect the suitability of your old car. Let's say you've been using a fuel-efficient, subcompact car all your single life; you will need a larger car when you get married or start having kids.

YOU MAY NEED a new car if you change occupations. For example, the vehicle you were using for daily commuting may not be suitable now that you're self-employed. You may need a large storage vehicle, like a pickup truck or S.U.V.

AND, should you leave a pastoral area to an urban district, where streets are narrow, a pickup truck or S.U.V. won't fit in. You will need a small, comfortable car.

JUST MAKE sure you can afford a car (and its added expenses) before purchasing or hurting your finances. It's okay if you can't afford one; several alternative options to owning a car are available. No problem if you don't have the money to throw at a car right now; you can save money to purchase it conveniently soon.

HERE, I want to show you a few alternatives to owning a car:

1. Public transportation.

YOU COULD USE a public vehicle to get to your destination. The cost of using public transportation is very affordable, though if you live in areas where efficient public transport is not accessible, you will struggle to move around.

. . .

2. Car-sharing clubs.

IF YOU HAVE any scheduled appointments, you can hire a car via a car-sharing club.

3. Ride with Uber *or* Lyft.

RIDING companies like Uber and Lyft can move you from one place to another. They are suitable for suburban and night travel.

4. Bicycles and walking.

SIMPLY WALKING or using a bike to get to nearby locations are more great options. You can walk or ride a bike to improve your health.

Should I Purchase a New or Used Car?

I had to answer this question many years ago when my crazy, fourteen-year-old van broke down, and I wondered whether to buy a new or used car. After I had test-driven a few cars, I asked myself whether I should go for a new or used one. I asked myself if I could afford a new car.

SINCE I HAD THE CASH, I went for it. Because most people around my age then couldn't afford a new car, I soon became the guy everyone talked about. I liked the frenzy but dared not tell anyone that the car drained all of my savings.

MAYBE I WOULD HAVE MADE a different or better choice if I had considered the pros and cons of buying a new or used car. So, before you decide on the vehicle to purchase, Weliver (2019) advises you to carefully analyze the benefits and drawbacks of new and used vehicles:

ADVANTAGES OF A NEW CAR:

1. Manufacturer warranty.
2. No prior owners, accidents, or mechanical faults.
3. Limited maintenance costs for two to three years.
4. Low financing rates.

Disadvantages of a new car:

1. Higher tax and insurance costs.
2. Unknown dependability for the model year.
3. Sudden devaluation.
4. Highly expensive.

Advantages of a used car:

1. Slower depreciation.
2. Lower tax and insurance costs.
3. Less costly.
4. Reliability data for the model year available from consumer reports.

Disadvantages of a used car:

1. Higher financing rates.
2. Unknown accident or mechanical record.
3. Higher maintenance costs.
4. Higher dealer markup.

I'm sure you can make a wise choice once you consider the merits and demerits of used and new cars. Again, base your selection on what you can afford, your personal preferences, and what's safe for you.

SHOULD you decide to purchase a used car, the following tips can be very useful:

1. Don't shop for the car until you know the price range for financing it.
2. Determine the total payments of the loan.
3. Grab a reliable car that will serve you for a few years.
4. Take a test drive.
5. Let a mechanic check the car.
6. See the car's history report.

PURCHASING a Car with Cash

YOU'RE GETTING a loan or paying with cash to purchase a car. If you have the full amount in cash, you will probably buy the car outright. Buying a car with cash means you can avoid the interest that comes with car loans. However, using your cash reserves to purchase a vehicle probably isn't right since that money could shift into your savings account.

. . .

USE PART of your savings to make a substantial down-payment if you don't have any leftover financial cushion – that way, you can have the auto loan and accrued interest reduced. But, if you have strong credit, which qualifies you for a low-interest car loan, you could use your savings to purchase the car. Again, since you have good credit, the dealer may give you cash-back offers and unique financing options.

LOOKING at the benefits and drawbacks of purchasing a car with cash can help you reach a reasonable decision (Brozic, 2020). Here are the two crucial benefits of buying a vehicle with cash:

1. It curbs overspending.

YOU CAN EASILY STICK to your budget when buying a car in cash. Let's say you've budgeted $25,000 for a car, for example, and in the course of the interaction, the dealer starts suggesting additional extras, like a heated steering wheel, all-weather floor mats, and a few splash guards. These add-ons could cost you an extra $2,000, but you can avoid them if you stick to your budget.

2. It averts interest payments.

YOU CAN AVOID interest if you purchase a car in cash. If you make a $5,000 down-payment for a $30,000 car, for example, you need a $25,000 auto loan to complete the transaction. With a 4.5 percent interest rate and 48-month repayment term, you will pay $2,364 interest. You can avoid this sum if you buy the car in cash.

You've seen the benefits of acquiring a car for cash. We will now consider the significant drawbacks:

3. It can drain your savings.

Buying a car with cash can drain all of your savings and make you incapable of dealing with potential emergencies.

4. It could stop you from achieving other financial goals.

Let's say you are contributing to a retirement account or building your emergency fund. You simply can't attain these goals if you use all of your money to purchase a car.

Opt for car financing if you can't purchase your dream car in cash.

How to Get Car Financing

These auto-financing tips from Weliver (2021) can help you obtain an auto loan to purchase your dream car:

.   .   .

1. Check your credit score and report before obtaining a car loan.

BAD CREDIT CAN'T STOP you from getting a car loan; it's just that you'll pay more if your credit isn't good enough. And, should you fail to meet up with the monthly repayment plan, the bank (or lender) can repossess the car.

LIKE MANY FINANCIAL TOOLS, *Credit Karma can be used to analyze and appreciate your credit score* to know if you can attain the most favorable car loan rates.

2. Obtain financial quotes if you don't have perfect credit.

PEOPLE with outstanding credit can access special dealership rates, but you have nothing to worry about if your credit isn't that good. Complete a credit application with an online lender if you hope to raise a car loan; you will learn the maximum amount of the loan and the interest rate once you have done so.

3. Keep the repayment term short.

A LONG-TERM LOAN attracts more interest than a short-term one. So, consider making the repayment term quick if you can afford it.

4. Put a 20 percent payment down (minimum).

. . .

I'M sure you won't like to owe more than the vehicle's current value, so make a minimum down-payment of 20 percent. The more, the better if you have the budget since it will lower your total interest.

5. Pay car fees, taxes, and miscellaneous expenses in cash.

DON'T GET a loan to finance sales tax, documentation fees, registration charges and related expenses.

Getting Married and Starting a Family

Marriage can change your financial, legal, and tax status, including your future choices. What your would-be spouse is bringing to the union may have a significant impact on your financial picture. So, if you hope to have an eventful marriage, you and your spouse must be on the same financial page. Why? Because money troubles top the chart of likely causes of divorce today. When you are on the same money page as your spouse, you can build a financially secure and healthy marriage. How can you achieve this? Have a financial talk with your spouse before you get married.

HERE'S how to make it happen:

1. Be open about your financial situation.

TALK FREELY about each other's assets, liabilities, and financial responsibilities. Get each other's credit scores and reports, and review your balance sheets together. Discuss potential concerns and find a way to deal with them.

2. Do a prenuptial agreement if one partner has more assets or earns more money than the other.

SHOULD DIVORCE OCCUR, such a treaty can safeguard premarital assets, solidify responsibility for acquired debts before marriage, and offer spousal support.

3. Devise a plan to improve each other's poor credit.

LIFE IS BETTER if you both have outstanding credit scores.

4. Set mutual financial objectives.

IF THERE ARE any questions you would like to discuss with your partner, write them down and talk about them.

5. Talk about how to merge your finances.

DISCUSS the money-managing strategy you guys are comfortable with. Agree on whether to set up a joint account or keep separate accounts. If the joint account works, decide the amount each person will contribute to the account monthly. If you're opting for individual accounts, decide who will be responsible for which particular expenses.

DON'T FORGET to talk about how to file taxes: will you file jointly or separately?

6. Plan your wedding and decide how to raise funds for the event.

CREATE a wedding budget and try to stick to it.

HONEST MONEY DISCUSSIONS can salvage a disastrous relationship and prevent a marriage from potentially ripping apart. Are there any other ways you could begin a financially stable marriage?

Starting a Family

Starting a family is an exciting, life-changing decision, but it comes with many financial obligations. You might have heard people say that the cost of purchasing a home amounts to a fortune; still, that's far below the cost of raising a child or two. For example, you will spend up to $227,000 to raise a child in the United States, excluding the child's college tuition.

I'VE ALWAYS TOLD young couples to build a family they can maintain. If it takes $227,000 to raise a child, how would you finance two or three kids? Consider these expenses before you start having kids:

- Childcare costs.
- Increase in regular expenses.
- Baby-proofing costs.
- Insurance needs.
- Documents which need to be updated, like wills, retirement plans and insurance policies.
- Education costs.

Are you still willing to be a parent now? Linton (2021) says that you aren't ready if you haven't hit the following money milestones:

1. Reliable career.

YOU MUST HAVE a stable job before becoming a parent – just make sure that the job can sustain your growing family. Identify and pursue careers that your children can maintain. Strive to earn a salary that can address the needs of your family.

2. Emergency fund.

UNEXPECTED EXPENSES CAN POP up in the family; as a parent, you need to be prepared to deal with emergencies each time they occur. That's where the emergency fund comes in. Make sure the fund has up to three- or six-months expenses.

3. Retirement plan.

. . .

THE COST of raising a child increases as the child grows. So, open a 401(k) or a Roth IRA account and start saving money. The fund will help you avoid the financial burden of retirement. Don't jump into marriage if you aren't contributing to a retirement plan.

4. College savings.

YOU AREN'T ready for marriage if you haven't started saving for college. The student loan debt issue continues to rise at an alarming rate every year, and, from the look of things, the problem won't turn around soon. Still, you can protect your future children from this hassle by saving for their college education now. That way, you will give them a financial edge when they eventually hit college age.

DON'T RUSH into starting a family without adequate preparation.

Financial Points to Evaluate Before Starting a Family

Starting a family can change everything about you, including your finances. Since you're leaving the singles' club, you have to modify your wants, needs, and expenses to suit your partner and kids (if you already have or will be having children). For example, you may have to purchase another car if your current vehicle isn't suitable for your family. Also, you will have to look elsewhere if your home doesn't have adequate space for your family. You're going to hurt your finances if you don't prepare financially before starting a family (Clarfeld, 2018).

· · ·

CONSIDER these financial steps if you hope to start and run a successful family:

1. Obtain wills and related documents.

I KNOW it's hard to think about the time you won't be around to attend to your children's needs, so address your estate matters now. Talk to an attorney if you don't have wills and relevant documents; you don't have to wait until you start having children. Should anything happen to you or your spouse, your children will be comfortable. I'm sure the joy of every parent is to see their children happy and safe.

APART FROM DRAFTING YOUR WILLS, the attorney should provide powers of attorney, living wills, healthcare proxies, and other vital documents.

MOST PEOPLE WON'T WANT to discuss their mortality, but that's a critical parenthood responsibility.

2. Create a new budget.

WHEN YOU START A NEW FAMILY, you have to modify your living costs, employment status, housing expenditures, childcare, and medical expenses. So, you've got to create a thoughtful budget to approximate your income to reach these daunting changes.

. . .

3. Identify the right life insurance.

MANY YOUNG PARENTS don't know the benefits of life insurance. Instead of concentrating on potential income providers, like life insurance, they focus on the amount they need to sustain their family lifestyle; they don't acquire substantial assets or get close to their maximum earning years. But, you should know that you can quickly pay down mortgages and debts, fund a child's education and maintain a family's lifestyle with life insurance.

HOWEVER, you may struggle to determine the insurance type to purchase since permanent coverage could slightly strain your family budget. Let an experienced insurance professional guide you through the available insurance policies. Then you can opt for the one which suits your family's needs.

4. Re-analyze your savings and investment plans.

START PRIORITIZING SAVING and investing your money if you haven't been doing so. You can't concentrate solely on saving and investments once you have a baby.

CONSIDER OPENING a savings account in U.G.M.A. or 529 plans to fund the education of your future children. Just make sure that you invest consistently, and remember to grow your emergency fund.

.   .   .

STARTING A FAMILY IS STRESSFUL, but it's a phase you will enjoy as a parent if you plan for it. You have to start planning for the future because you will probably start a family someday.

I'VE ALREADY TOLD you that the future is all about money. That's why this chapter has all the tips you need to make reasonable adulting decisions. Start saving and investing your money right now if you want to build a great future for yourself and your family.

CONCLUSION

"Personal Finance for Teens and College Students" is a money-management guide for teens and college students who hope to enjoy their lives and attain their financial goals. The eight-chapter book provides great tips, insights, and strategies for setting unique financial objectives and how to reach them with commitment and attention.

The key highlights of this book include:

1. Logical steps for creating budgets, sticking to them and growing your money
2. Helpful tips on creating a bank account, analyzing bank statements and avoiding unnecessary bank fees
3. Practical guides on differentiating wants from needs, exhibiting critical financial skills, and attaining mindful spending habits
4. Good techniques for credit card use, minimizing debts, and improving one's credit score

5. Sensible investment options to exploit to sustain, maximize and grow your money
6. Creative ideas for building additional sources of income, to attain financial freedom
7. Useful tips on filing taxes and using tax credit
8. Efficient strategies for making profitable adulting decisions

As you strive to stay on track to improve your personal finances, keep in mind that you can do it if you just try. If you take the first initial step forward, you will be in the position to achieve your present and future financial goals. So, stay focused, persistent, determined and consistent and you should be on your way to staying in control of your personal finances.

Rest assured that you will gain the required tools and resources to achieve your heart's goals. Don't hesitate to utilize the money-making strategies you have already learnt in the book.

Who says you can't be successful with money and life?

I would like to hear from you. If you enjoyed reading this book, kindly leave me a review through your favorite online book retailer.

Many Thanks.

CPSIA information can be obtained
at www.ICGtesting.com
Printed in the USA
LVHW080332060922
727606LV00014B/1149